PRAISE FOR
FROM BREAKDOWNS TO BREAKTHROUGHS

"*From Breakdowns to Breakthroughs* gives teachers practical, trauma-responsive strategies they can use right away. Fields and Davis remind us that behavior is communication, and their Hacks provide clear steps for creating classrooms built on safety, connection, and hope. This book not only equips educators with immediate tools but also reinforces a truth I deeply believe: relationships are the key to lasting change. A valuable resource for any educator committed to reaching every student."

— DR. BRAD JOHNSON, #3 GLOBAL GURU IN EDUCATION, INTERNATIONAL SPEAKER, AND AUTHOR OF *ROOM 212* AND *RESILIENT STUDENTS*

"Infused with hard-won wisdom, this book by seasoned teachers Katie Fields and Jill M. Davis shares discipline and guidance Hacks that will help you create a more peaceful classroom where children can flourish academically and emotionally. Based on solid principles of neuroscience and human development, the ideas they present not only apply to children who have experienced maltreatment and trauma but to all students. And there are practical steps you can implement tomorrow in elementary, middle school, and high school classrooms. A helpful read for all teachers seeking new tools to meet the challenges of classroom life."

— DR. BARBARA SORRELS, 25-YEAR EDUCATOR AND UNIVERSITY PROFESSOR, EXECUTIVE DIRECTOR OF THE INSTITUTE FOR CHILDHOOD EDUCATION IN TULSA, FOUNDER OF CONNECTED KIDS, AND AUTHOR OF *REACHING AND TEACHING CHILDREN EXPOSED TO TRAUMA* AND *TRAUMA-SENSITIVE CARE FOR INFANTS, TODDLERS, AND TWO-YEAR-OLDS*

"What an honor to be asked to write a review for this amazing resource for educators. These extraordinary authors provide us with an invaluable resource, calling out what is real in education and providing us with trauma-responsive ways to address it. The layout is perfect! I love how they broke down each Hack to provide us with real-life examples, critical reminders of what education is about, the solution to address the issue, and strategies we can do both in the moment and in the long term. I especially love the section on how to address the pushback, and the practical tidbits and refreshing reframes resonated deeply with me. This is a resource that will truly help us improve the work we are doing with students, staff, and families. Thank you, Dr. Fields and Dr. Davis, for providing such a valuable book. It truly is a must-read!"

— Dr. Kristin Souers, trainer, consultant, and coauthor of Fostering Resilient Learners and Relationship, Responsibility, and Regulation

"I thoroughly enjoyed reading *From Breakdowns to Breakthroughs*! The writing is so clear and leans far into practice while staying solidly attuned to theory. As I read, I kept thinking, 'They put that idea so succinctly,' 'I have to remember how they phrased that,' and 'Why didn't I think of that in my classroom?' In fact, I underlined forty-seven ideas and quotes ... it's that good. As Fields and Davis remind us, strategies that are necessary for our underserved, exploited, and traumatized students are invaluable for the entire class, regardless of their backgrounds. Every school, every student, and every teacher will thrive and grow by reading this book."

— Jeffrey Benson, fifty-plus-year educator, consultant, presenter, and international author of numerous articles and books, including Hacking School Discipline Together

From Breakdowns to Breakthroughs by Dr. Katie Fields and Dr. Jill M. Davis should be required reading for every prospective and veteran teacher, but especially for those who are emergency certified or adjuncts. Out with the old-school 'this is how it's always been done' classroom management, and in with a trauma-responsive framework built on compassion and connection, which leads to fewer classroom behavior issues and real student achievement.

"Fields and Davis remind us to shift the question from 'What's wrong with you?' to 'What happened to you?' I wish I'd read this book before my first year of teaching, as I would've been more

effective with just this one shift in perspective. The ten practical Hacks give teachers real strategies such as moving away from shame-based behavior charts, looking at a child as more than a test score, prioritizing relationships, really listening to students, and integrating social-emotional regulation support. These strategies can turn any classroom into a safe learning space for students and teachers.

"This isn't just another book about discipline alternatives; it's a call for more empathy in education across the board. It's also a blueprint for all public education stakeholders because, if we really want to help every student feel seen, safe, *and* ready to learn, this engaging book shows us how."

— JACOB ROSECRANTS, OKLAHOMA STATE REPRESENTATIVE
AND AUTHOR OF HB 1569, "THE PLAY TO LEARN ACT"

From Breakdowns to Breakthroughs is the book every exhausted teacher, every worried parent, and every child advocate has secretly wished for—and now it's here. Katie Fields and Jill M. Davis have written a guide that is equal parts research-based, practical, and compassionate, with just enough honesty to make you nod your head and say, 'Yes, that's my classroom … my kitchen table … my after-school program … my Sunday school class.'

"No longer do educators, parents, and advocates have to wonder, 'What do I do with a child who …?' Each chapter moves seamlessly from real-world vignettes to clear explanations and, most impor-tantly, to a blueprint that offers strategies for tomorrow, next week, and long-term success. These blueprints are more than tips; they are lifelines that make the work feel possible, even in the busiest and most challenging environments. Fields and Davis not only help us understand why children struggle, melt down over a pencil, or unravel during math, but they also show us how to respond in ways that restore dignity, safety, and connection without losing our sanity.

"The genius of this book is its humanity. Fields and Davis

remind us that behavior is communication, and our task is not to win power struggles but to listen for the story underneath. That message alone has the power to transform classrooms, homes, programs, and dinner tables everywhere.

"Whether you're a teacher Googling 'How to survive teaching' at 2 a.m., a parent wondering if you're the only one whose child has emotional avalanches over socks, or a teacher educator preparing future professionals for tomorrow's classrooms, this book is for you. *From Breakdowns to Breakthroughs* is as practical as it is profound, as hopeful as it is honest, and both laugh-out-loud funny and deeply moving. It should be required reading for every educator, every parent, and every leader who believes that education can be both academically rigorous and profoundly humane."
— DR. VICKIE E. LAKE, ASSOCIATE DEAN, PROFESSOR, TEACHER EDUCATOR, AND AUTHOR OF *FROM ABD TO PHD AND EDD: NAVIGATING THE FINAL STRETCH OF YOUR DOCTORAL JOURNEY*

"As a school psychologist, I am always looking for practices that improve learning for every student while especially protecting access and dignity for students with disabilities. This book delivers exactly that and more. It is practical, strength-based, and built for real classrooms. Teachers will find guidance they can use right away that makes students feel safer, more seen, and more ready to learn. Whether or not a child has experienced trauma, the approaches in this book support well-being and keep instruction moving. I recommend it for teachers, special educators, and anyone dedicated to ensuring students learn in psychologically safe spaces."
— DR. KELSIE REED, NATIONALLY CERTIFIED SCHOOL PSYCHOLOGIST, COAUTHOR OF *HACKING DEFICIT THINKING*, AND FOUNDER OF STRENGTH-BASED COLLECTIVE

"The most requested topic I receive for professional development training is classroom management. Educators are increasingly aware that learning doesn't happen in isolation from lived experience, especially for children carrying the invisible weight of trauma. This book is a powerful guide and compassionate companion for teachers seeking to respond, rather than react, to the emotional realities their students bring to school each day. By offering practical strategies and insights rooted in trauma-informed care, this work invites educators to see behavior through a new lens: not as defiance but as communication. It encourages teachers to shift from traditional classroom management models to ones built on connection, trust, and emotional safety. With actionable tips on how to create responsive learning environments, this book equips educators to meet all children where they are. This is more than a teaching manual; it's a call to transform our classrooms into spaces of healing, resilience, and hope."

— DR. KIMBERLY PHILLIPS, EARLY CHILDHOOD PROFESSOR, CASA VOLUNTEER, AND ADVOCATE FOR ALL

"In my thirty-two years as an educator, I've learned that every child has a unique 'popping point.' Like popcorn, some kids burst open easily, while others need time and patience to thrive. Our mission as educators is to create the right conditions for every single child to succeed.

"*From Breakdowns to Breakthroughs* beautifully illustrates this truth. Authors Katie Fields and Jill M. Davis remind us that a child's behavior is a form of communication, especially for those with unseen struggles. The authors' compassionate, practical strategies echo what I once called 'hugging a porcupine': giving kids the love and support they need, even when it feels challenging.

"This book is a powerful guide for anyone dedicated to serving every child. It belongs in the hands of every educator who wants to move beyond managing behavior and start transforming lives."

— ROB MILLER, SUPERINTENDENT (RETIRED), BIXBY PUBLIC SCHOOLS, BIXBY, OKLAHOMA

"One example of why I find this book especially powerful and informative is that it calls out a practice so common in schools: public behavior charts. The authors make a compelling case that these systems shame children, undermine learning, and retraumatize our most vulnerable students. Katie Fields and Jill M. Davis don't just critique the problem but also offer clear, practical solutions (such as private conversations, restorative practices, and ways to build intrinsic motivation) that honor student dignity while still maintaining accountability. As an educator and principal, this resonates with me deeply; true growth comes when students feel safe, respected, and supported, not when their struggles are put on display. This book is a tremendous resource and a wonderful, useful tool for all educators, counselors, classroom teachers, parents, and school leaders."

— DR. BARBARA JONES, ASSOCIATE PROFESSOR OF EDUCATIONAL LEADERSHIP/SCHOOL ADMINISTRATION, NORTHEASTERN STATE UNIVERSITY

FROM
BREAKDOWNS
TO
BREAKTHROUGHS

10 SIMPLE STRATEGIES TO
REDUCE DISRUPTIONS AND CREATE
TRAUMA-RESPONSIVE CLASSROOMS

HACK™
Learning
SERIES

KATIE FIELDS
& JILL M. DAVIS

From Breakdowns to Breakthroughs
© 2025 by Times 10 Publications
Highland Heights, OH 44143 USA
Website: 10publications.com

All web links in this book are correct as of the publication date but
may have become inactive or otherwise modified since that time. Name
brands should not be considered endorsements by the author or Times 10
Publications.

Cover and Interior Design by Steven Plummer
Project Management and Editing by Regina Bell
Copyediting by Jennifer Jas

Paperback ISBN: 978-1-956512-74-8
eBook ISBN: 978-1-956512-76-2
Hardcover ISBN: 978-1-956512-75-5

Library of Congress Cataloging-in-Publication Data is available for this
title.

First Printing: October 2025

Dedicated to you, the educator reading this book with hope in your heart and a willingness to grow, and to the children whose lives—and the lives of generations to come—will forever be changed by your commitment to trauma-responsive practices.

TABLE OF CONTENTS

INTRODUCTION

MOVE FROM ADD-ON TO INVESTMENT

Integrate Trauma-Responsive Practices for Thriving Classroom Communities

*The child who is not embraced by the village
will burn it down to feel its warmth.*
— AFRICAN PROVERB

WHAT IF ALL our training about classroom management is based on a fundamental misunderstanding? What if "misbehavior" isn't about behavior at all, but about communication?

You've seen them. The student who melts down over minor changes, the child who can't sit still, and the kid who argues about everything. You've tried behavior charts, consequences, and rewards. You've implemented the latest classroom management system, sent students to the office, called parents or guardians at home, and maybe even Googled "how to survive teaching" at 2 a.m. Some days, you've probably wondered whether you're cut out for this profession.

But what if the problem isn't the child? What if it's our approach?

When children don't feel embraced by their classroom community, they will find ways to get our attention, even if those ways look like disruption, defiance, or withdrawal. They're not trying to make our lives difficult. They're trying to communicate essential messages about their needs, their fears, or their pain. The question isn't whether we're listening; it's whether we know how to hear what they're saying.

WELCOME TO YOUR MOST IMPORTANT INVESTMENT

If you've chosen to read this book, chances are you've experienced the frustration of trying to help a challenging student. Maybe it is the student who breaks down every Monday morning, the child who refuses to participate, or the kid who seems to carry the weight of the world on his shoulders. You've probably wondered why traditional discipline approaches make you feel like you're swimming upstream, why behavior charts don't change behavior in the long term, and why your most challenging kids often seem to need a level of attention that you weren't taught to give. You're not alone.

Traditional classroom management was designed for a different time, back when we understood less about trauma, stress, and the developing brain. We now know that at least half of all children have experienced a form of trauma, and that's likely an underestimate. For many students, especially those in foster care, the percentages are even higher. What does this mean for your classroom? Trauma-responsive practices aren't specialty interventions for a few students; they're essential teaching strategies that benefit everyone.

Trauma-responsive practices don't add more to your already full plate or create "extras" for you to squeeze in between math and reading. We know you're already juggling curriculum demands, assessment requirements, and the seventeen other initiatives your district has rolled out this year. Too many educational approaches ask teachers to layer new strategies on top of existing practices without addressing the fundamental challenges. This book offers a different method. Trauma-responsive practices are an investment in all of your teaching practices, making your current efforts more effective rather than adding to your workload.

An investment in classroom management. When students feel safe and understood, 90 percent of behavior problems disappear before they start. You'll spend less time managing crises and more time teaching.

An investment in students' futures. Children who learn they're worthy of patience and understanding become adults who believe in their potential. You're not just teaching content; you're healing wounds and building resilience.

An investment in your sanity. Teaching becomes joyful again when you stop fighting against students and start working with them. (And yes, you'll want to go to work on Monday mornings again.) Understanding behavior as communication, rather than defiance, shifts your entire classroom experience.

An investment in time. Having trauma-responsive practices in place affords you more teaching time in the long run. Prevention is more efficient than reaction.

UNDERSTANDING THE FOUNDATION

Before we dive into the Hacks, let's establish the crucial groundwork. When we talk about trauma-responsive teaching, we're not solely talking about children who've experienced what we think of as "big-T" Trauma: abuse, neglect, and major life events. We're also addressing what researchers call "little-t" trauma: divorce, moving frequently, chronic stress, family financial struggles, medical issues, and simply living in an unpredictable world.

All trauma has one common factor: it rewires the developing brain for survival rather than learning. When children are stuck in fight, flight, freeze, or fawn mode, the parts of their brains responsible for attention, memory, and logical thinking go offline. These kids aren't *choosing* to be difficult. Their nervous systems are doing what they're designed to do when they perceive danger.

Here's where it gets more complex. Children who have been in the foster care system experience what we call "trauma-*plus*," which describes the compounding factors that amplify trauma's impact, specifically for children in the foster care system. These children often experience the initial trauma that led to their removal from home, plus the compounding losses that follow. They may lose their school, friends, siblings, neighborhood, church, personal belongings, extracurricular activities, and their entire support network. When behavioral challenges emerge at school (which is normal for children processing trauma), the issues can escalate into conflicts that contribute to what's called "disrupting placement," meaning the child is removed from the foster home. Then the cycle repeats with new trauma, new losses, a new school, new teachers, and new everything. Children who have been in the foster care system can experience multiple disruptions, each one compounding the original trauma with fresh losses and instability.

This reality means these children have learned that "permanent" might not mean permanent, that relationships can end without warning, and that adults, even caring ones, might not stay. For many students who have been in the foster care system, their teachers become the most consistent adults in their lives. This makes your response to their behavior absolutely critical. How you choose to respond to this child's challenging behavior can either escalate the situation, potentially contributing to placement disruption, or de-escalate it, providing the stability and understanding they desperately need in order to heal and grow. Teachers wield enormous power in the trajectory of a foster child's life, often without realizing it.

THE NEUROSCIENCE THAT CHANGES EVERYTHING

Understanding trauma's impact on the brain isn't just academic; it completely transforms how we respond to student behavior. When a child's amygdala (the brain's alarm system) is activated by stress or a perceived threat, the prefrontal cortex (responsible for reasoning, planning, and emotional regulation) goes offline. In this state, traditional consequences and logical reasoning don't work because students cannot access the parts of their brains that would make sense of them.

This scenario is why time-outs often backfire with kids affected by trauma. Isolation triggers the abandonment fears that trauma has already activated. You can probably see why behavior charts can retraumatize rather than motivate. Public tracking of behavior creates the shame and exposure that trauma survivors have learned to fear. "Logical consequences" often feel anything but logical to students whose logic centers are offline.

When we understand this neuroscience, we shift our understanding and our actions. We stop thinking about a student in terms of "What's wrong with you?" and start thinking, "What happened to you?" We stop trying to punish trauma responses and start helping students regulate their nervous systems. We stop seeing "misbehavior" as defiance and start seeing it as communication.

WHY THIS APPROACH BENEFITS ALL STUDENTS

Here's a crucial element of this discussion: Trauma-responsive practices aren't only for students who've experienced trauma. They create classroom environments where all children thrive. When we design learning spaces that account for different nervous system needs, provide predictability and choice, focus on strengths rather than deficits, and prioritize relationships, we're creating conditions that support every learner.

The student who has never experienced trauma still benefits from feeling seen and valued. The typically developing child still thrives in an environment that offers choice and honors student interests. The academically gifted student still needs emotional safety and authentic relationships. Trauma-responsive teaching is about creating the optimal conditions for *all* brains to learn and grow.

DIFFERENCES BETWEEN BEING INFORMED, SENSITIVE, AND RESPONSIVE

As you begin this journey, understand the distinction between being trauma-informed, trauma-sensitive, and trauma-responsive:

- **Trauma-informed** means you understand that trauma exists and affects learning. You know the statistics and recognize the signs.

- **Trauma-sensitive** means you avoid practices that might retraumatize students. You eliminate public behavior charts and think twice about assignments that might trigger painful memories.

- **Trauma-responsive** means you actively create conditions that support healing and growth. You don't just avoid harm; you intentionally foster resilience, connection, and empowerment.

This book will guide you to move beyond simply being trauma-informed to becoming genuinely trauma-responsive in your daily practice. You don't have to be perfect at this work. You have to be willing to see your students' behavior as their best attempt to communicate an important message to you. Transformation begins when you are willing to truly listen, to hear the need behind the behavior, and to understand the communication behind the challenge.

We wrote this book based on our experiences as educators, parents, and advocates. We've studied the research, read books, attended professional development sessions and conferences, observed in classrooms, and visited with many professionals, both in and outside of education, to gain as much knowledge as possible about this topic. We acknowledge and appreciate all these sources that gave us the background knowledge that made it possible for us to share the practical steps with you.

The ten Hacks (chapters) in this book are designed to be practical, immediately implementable, and transformative. Each Hack begins with a vignette, inspired by a composite of real classroom experiences, that illustrates authentic challenges teachers face. The vignette leads into *The Problem* followed by *The Hack*, a clear strategy you can apply to solve it. Next is the *What You Can Do Tomorrow* section with actionable tips you can implement right away, followed by *A Blueprint for Full Implementation*, listing the long-term steps to make this Hack stick. To further support you, the *Overcoming Pushback* section lists common objections along with suggestions for navigating them. In *The Hack in Action*, we share representative scenarios using invented names that illustrate the diverse individuals in a typical classroom. And finally, *Reflection Questions* invite you to examine your practices and deepen your understanding.

You don't need to implement all ten Hacks at once. Start with the one that resonates most strongly with your current challenges, or begin with the simple steps you can take tomorrow. Small changes in how you see and respond to students can create profound ripple effects.

The child who is not embraced by the village will indeed burn it down to feel its warmth. But when we learn to embrace our most challenging students, when we create classrooms that feel like villages of belonging, a beautiful shift happens: these children become the light that illuminates possibilities for everyone.

Your classroom can be that village. Your response can be that embrace. And the investment you make in understanding and supporting your most vulnerable students will pay dividends in their lives and in the lives of every child you teach.

Let's begin.

HACK 1

REFRAME AND RESPOND

See Behavior as Communication
and Plan Thoughtful Responses

*Children do well if they can. If they're not doing
well, it's because they lack the skills to do well,
not because they lack the will to do well.*
— DR. ROSS GREENE, CLINICAL PSYCHOLOGIST

THE OFFICE REFERRAL was already half-written when eight-year-old Marcus launched himself under his desk for the third time that morning. "Defiant," Mrs. Rodriguez was ready to write. "Disruptive." "Refuses to follow directions." The usual suspects in our behavior vocabulary. But she felt the need to pause. Maybe it was the way Marcus pressed his hands against his ears or how his eyes darted toward the hallway every time footsteps went by. Instead of reaching for the referral slip, she crouched next to his desk.

"Hey, buddy," she whispered. "What's happening?"

Through tears, Marcus whispered back, "My mom said she might not pick me up today. She said maybe my dad would come instead." Suddenly, everything clicked. Marcus's parents were in the midst of a messy divorce. His dad, whom he hadn't seen in months, was supposed to have supervised visits that kept getting canceled. The "defiance" wasn't defiance at all; it was terror. Marcus was hiding under his desk because he was afraid his world was about to crumble again.

What if Mrs. Rodriguez had sent that referral? What if she had labeled him "difficult" and moved on? She would have missed the real message Marcus was desperately trying to communicate: *I'm scared, I'm overwhelmed, and I need someone to see that I'm drowning.* That moment changed how Mrs. Rodriguez saw student behavior. It taught her that behind every "misbehavior" is a child trying to give us a critical message about what they are experiencing. Educators must listen and hear what our students are really saying.

THE PROBLEM: WE'RE MANAGING BEHAVIOR INSTEAD OF UNDERSTANDING IT

Walk into many teacher prep programs, and you'll learn about behavior charts, consequence ladders, and the importance of "being consistent." You'll practice your stern teacher voice and learn phrases like, "I need you to make better choices." But here's what you probably didn't learn: Most of what we call "misbehavior" isn't about behavior at all. It's about communication.

When trauma enters a child's life, whether it's big-T Trauma like abuse or neglect or little-t trauma like divorce, moving, or chronic stress, it rewires the child's developing brain. The part responsible for logical thinking goes offline while the part responsible for survival kicks into overdrive. These kids aren't choosing to be difficult any more than you choose to jump when someone sneaks up behind you. Their nervous systems are stuck in alarm mode, constantly scanning for danger.

But here's the kicker: We adults often interpret these trauma responses as deliberate misbehavior. Students who can't sit still aren't "hyperactive"; they're hypervigilant, always ready to flee. Children who argue with every instruction aren't "oppositional"; they're trying to maintain some sense of control in a world that feels chaotic. Kids who shut down completely aren't "lazy"; they're overwhelmed and protecting themselves the only way they know how.

The field of education has created a system where educators are essentially punishing children for having a normal trauma response. It's like we're giving students detention for bleeding when they're cut. The behavior is a symptom, not the problem.

EDUCATORS ARE ESSENTIALLY PUNISHING CHILDREN FOR HAVING A NORMAL TRAUMA RESPONSE. IT'S LIKE WE'RE GIVING STUDENTS DETENTION FOR BLEEDING WHEN THEY'RE CUT.

Also, let's talk about that phrase we love to throw around: "They just want attention." Well, yeah, of course they do. Attention from caring adults is a basic human need, especially for kids whose attachment systems have been disrupted by trauma. When we say, "They just want attention" as if it's a character flaw, we're essentially saying, "How dare this child need connection with a caring adult." Put that way, it sounds ridiculous, doesn't it?

This scenario is especially true for children who have been in the foster care system, who may have experienced multiple placement changes and disrupted attachments with caregivers. These children have learned that adults might not stick around and relationships can end without warning. When they seek extra attention or connection from a teacher, they're not being "needy" or "attention-seeking." They're trying to form a stable, caring relationship that their developing brains desperately need. For many children who have been in the foster care system, teachers might be the most consistent adults in their lives.

Here's what complicates this further. Children who have experienced trauma may be operating at half their chronological age emotionally. That "mature" ten-year-old who helps take care of siblings at home? She might have the emotional regulation skills of a five-year-old when she's stressed. That seventh-grader who seems so "together"? Inside, he might be a scared second-grader just trying to survive.

The problem worsens when we engage in power struggles with children. Newsflash! You never win a power struggle with a child. Even when you "win," you lose because you've just taught a vulnerable kid that relationships are about dominance rather than connection. And guess what trauma teaches kids? It teaches them that the world is unsafe and they can't trust adults. Every time we escalate behavior issues, we're confirming the student's worst fears about the world.

Think about the last time you had a bad day. Maybe you were short with your partner, snapped at a colleague, or cried for a minor reason. Did someone send you to the principal's office? Did they make you flip your behavior card to red? Of course not, because as adults, we understand that behavior is often a reflection of one's internal state, not one's character.

Yet somehow, we expect children, whose brains won't be fully developed for another decade or two, to have better emotional regulation than we do. We expect them to "leave their problems at home" and show up ready to learn, even when their home lives are chaotic, scary, or unpredictable. We expect them to "make good choices" when their trauma-affected brains are incapable of accessing the prefrontal cortex, the part that makes good choices.

The truth is that most challenging behavior isn't about the moment it happens; it's about all the moments that led up to it. It's about the unseen burdens children carry, some light as feathers and others heavy as rocks. And until we start seeing behavior as communication rather than defiance, we'll continue to miss the real messages our most vulnerable students are trying to send us.

THE HACK: REFRAME AND RESPOND

So, what's the solution? It starts with a simple but revolutionary shift in perspective. Instead of asking, "What's wrong with you?" ask, "What happened to you?" Instead of "How do I make this behavior stop?" ask, "What is this behavior trying to tell me?" This line of questioning is about becoming a detective, a translator, and a safe harbor in the storm of a child's life. It's about understanding that the most "difficult" students are often the ones who need us the most.

The Core Strategy: Listen to the Behavior

Every behavior has a message. Students who are always out of their seats might be saying, "My body feels unsafe sitting still." Children who argue about everything might be thinking, "I need to feel some control in my life." Kids who shut down during math may be saying, "This reminds me of when my dad used to yell at me about homework."

Here's your new superpower: pattern recognition. Instead of reacting to each behavior incident as an isolated event, start looking for patterns. What time of day do meltdowns happen? What activities trigger shutdowns? What days of the week are hardest? These patterns are breadcrumbs that lead you to the real issue.

Maya, a second-grader in a colleague's class, had epic meltdowns every Tuesday. *Every* Tuesday. The teacher tried behavior charts, extra recess, and any other tactic she could think of. Nothing worked until she realized the pattern. Tuesday was Maya's mom's day for supervised visits. The visits kept getting canceled, but Maya didn't know whether she'd see her mom that day until she got to school, and her anxiety had nowhere to go. Once our colleague figured that out, she created a Tuesday morning check-in routine that gave Maya a way to express her worries before they exploded into problematic behavior.

Look Beyond the Surface

Every child walks into your classroom carrying an invisible backpack filled with their experiences. Some backpacks are light and packed with love, stability, and encouragement. Others are so heavy with trauma, stress, and responsibility that it's a miracle the child can walk at all.

Before you react to a troublesome behavior, pause and consider: What might be in this child's backpack today? Did he eat breakfast? Get enough sleep? Are her parents fighting? Is there drama with friends? Are they worried about something at home? Sometimes, the "disrespectful" behavior is the child's way to try to manage an overwhelming internal experience.

Kids communicate with their whole bodies, especially when they're dysregulated. That fidgety student isn't trying to annoy you; her nervous system is trying to regulate itself through movement. The child who keeps looking toward the door isn't necessarily ready to escape. He's unconsciously checking the exits because trauma taught him to have a plan, just in case.

Learn to read the nonverbal indicators like tight shoulders, clenched fists, rapid breathing, and darting eyes. These signals are your early warning system. When you see these signs, that's your cue to move closer (literally and figuratively), get down to the student's eye level or lower, soften your voice, and offer connection before correction. Towering over a dysregulated child, even unintentionally, can feel threatening to a nervous system that's already on high alert. Instead, crouch down, sit nearby, or find a way to make yourself physically smaller. This shift in positioning signals safety and tells the child's brain, "I'm not a threat. I'm here to help."

Build Relationships During the Calm

Relationship-building doesn't happen during crisis moments. You can't make deposits in the relationship bank account when everyone's emotionally overdrawn. The magic happens in the quiet moments, like the two minutes before class starts, the casual conversation during transition time, and the genuine interest in the students' weekend activities.

One middle school teacher we know greets every student at the door with personal comments. "How's your sister feeling?" "Did your mom's interview go well?" "I saw your goal in the soccer game!" These tiny moments of connection become the foundation that holds everything else together when life gets tough.

It's crucial that you develop relationships during the calm moments because that's when both the teacher's and the student's brains are in a state where connection is possible. When a child is dysregulated or in a crisis, the brain shifts out of logic mode and goes into survival mode. In this state, even small stressors can feel overwhelming or threatening. The child cannot form new positive associations or memories about relationships.

Think of it like trying to teach someone to swim while they are drowning. The person will not remember your swimming tips because their energy is focused on not going under. Similarly, a child in emotional crisis can't absorb your care and concern because their nervous system is screaming, *"Danger!"*

During calm moments, both you and the student can access the parts of your brains responsible for connection, building trust, and forming positive memories. These peaceful interactions create a relationship bank account that you can draw from during difficult times. When a crisis does hit, the child's brain has stored memories of you as a safe person, which helps the child regulate faster and trust your support.

It's also when you can learn who the student is as a person with interests, fears, hopes, and family dynamics. This crucial information helps you understand the student's behavior patterns.

What does this look like across different grade levels? The specifics matter because a genuine connection with a kindergartner looks different from establishing trust with a high schooler.

Elementary (PreK–5): These students often wear their hearts on their sleeves, making relationship-building more straightforward but no less critical. Try greeting each child by name as they enter, taking note of small details, such as new haircuts or favorite shirts. During transitions, ask about their pets, siblings, or weekend adventures. Create special jobs that give you one-on-one time. "Can you help me organize these books while everyone else lines up?" or "Would you be my special messenger to the office?" These moments may seem casual, but they inspire powerful connections.

One second-grade teacher keeps a small notebook where she jots down personal details students share, such as "Emma's cat had kittens," "Omar loves Pokémon," and "Zoe's grandma is visiting." She reviews it weekly and follows up. "How are those kittens doing?" These tiny check-ins tell students their lives matter to you beyond academics.

Middle school (6–8): Relationship-building gets trickier here because students are simultaneously craving adult connection and pushing boundaries. The key is showing genuine interest without being intrusive. Comment on their interests, such as: "I saw that the band you mentioned is coming to town," or "How's that book series you're reading?" Share appropriate pieces of your own life, such as: "Group projects used to stress me out, too, but I figured out ways to make them easier," or "My dog also hates baths."

Stand by your door between classes and offer genuine compliments, such as, "Your presentation yesterday was really thoughtful," or "I noticed you helped Felix with that math problem. That was kind." Middle schoolers desperately need to know they're seen as good humans, not only for their behavior problems or test scores.

High school (9–12): Teenagers can smell fake from a mile away, so authenticity is key. Show up to their games, plays, or concerts when possible. Remember what they're stressed about. "How did that job interview go?" or "Is your mom feeling better?" Acknowledge their growing independence. "What do you think we should do about this situation?" or "I value your perspective on this."

High schoolers also need to see you as human. Share your learning struggles. "I'm trying to figure out this new technology, too," or "I still make mistakes even though I am an adult." This vulnerability builds bridges rather than walls.

Universal strategies across all ages: Learn the correct pronunciation of every student's name, and use it frequently. Remember important events in their lives, and follow up. Notice positive changes. "You seem more confident in Spanish lately," or "I've noticed how thoughtful you've been with your classmates." Create rituals that connect: maybe it's a special handshake, a Friday check-in circle, or sharing one positive experience that happened each week.

We're not trying to be our students' friend or therapist, but rather a safe, consistent adult who sees them as whole human beings worthy of respect and care.

Don't Take It Personally

This concept is hard, especially when a kid is screaming that she hates you or that you're the worst teacher ever. But here's the truth: It's never about you. That child isn't angry at you person-ally—she's angry at the situation, her powerlessness, and her fear. You happen to be the safe adult in the room, which means she trusts you enough to fall apart in front of you.

One teacher we know keeps a note on his desk that states, "It's not happening *to* me; it's happening *in front of* me so I can respond with compassion." That's a game-changing message.

Think of it as an honor, contrary to how it feels in the moment. That child could shut down, run away, or internalize the bad thoughts. Instead, he's communicating his pain to you. He's giving you the chance to help.

No child wakes up thinking, "You know what sounds fun? Having a complete meltdown in science class today!" Challenging behavior is never the child's first choice—it's their last resort. It means all their other coping strategies have failed, and they've got nothing left.

When we remember that the behavior isn't intentional, it becomes much easier to respond with curiosity rather than frustration.

Check Your Own Backpack

Here's a fact they don't teach in most education programs: your own emotional baggage affects how you interpret and respond to student behavior. Every teacher walks into the classroom car-rying an invisible backpack filled with past experiences, current stressors, personal triggers, and unmet needs. When we're not aware of what's in our backpacks, it can hijack our abilities to see our students clearly.

Think about it. That student who talks back might remind you of your defiant younger brother, causing you to react more harshly than the situation warrants. The child who seems "manipulative" might trigger memories of feeling controlled in your childhood, leading you to see manipulation instead of a scared kid trying to meet critical needs. The student who shuts down completely might frustrate you because you're an external processor who needs to talk things through.

Your current life circumstances matter, too. Are you dealing with family stress, financial worries, or health concerns? Are you overwhelmed by administrative demands, difficult colleagues, or a lack of support? When our nervous systems are activated, we're much more likely to interpret neutral behaviors as threatening and respond from our fight-or-flight mode rather than from a place of wisdom and compassion.

> **WHEN YOU CAN STAY REGULATED AND RESPONSIVE RATHER THAN REACTIVE, YOU CREATE A SENSE OF SAFETY THAT PROMOTES HEALING AND LEARNING.**

Here's a quick self-check you can do when you feel your emotions rising in response to student behavior. Pause and ask yourself, "What's happening inside me right now?" Notice your physical sensations. Is your jaw clenched? Are your shoulders tight? Is your heart racing? These are clues that a trigger in your own backpack has been activated.

Then ask, "What is this reminding me of?" Maybe the student's eye-rolling reminds you of being dismissed as a child. Perhaps the child's arguing triggers your need to be right or in control. Sometimes, the behavior that bothers us the most in students is a behavior we struggle with ourselves or learned to suppress in our childhood.

Finally, ask, "What does this child need from me right now?" This question helps you shift from your emotional reaction back to your role as the caring adult in the room. It's not about suppressing your feelings or pretending they don't matter. It's about recognizing when your personal biases or assumptions are

31

interfering with your ability to see and respond to what's happening with your students.

The most self-aware teachers aren't those who never get triggered; they're the ones who notice when they are triggered and pause to choose their response rather than react automatically. Modeling this kind of emotional regulation is incredibly powerful for students, especially those who struggle with their own big emotions.

Taking care of your emotional well-being isn't selfish; it's essential for being the kind of teacher your students need. When you can stay regulated and responsive rather than reactive, you create a sense of safety that promotes healing and learning.

WHAT **YOU** CAN DO TOMORROW

Feeling overwhelmed by the idea of completely transforming your approach to behavior? Start small. You can implement these shifts immediately and make a significant difference in how you see and respond to challenging behavior. Remember, you don't need to overhaul everything at once—even small changes in your perspective and response can create profound impacts on your most vulnerable students.

- **Prepare students for changes:** Trauma thrives on unpredictability, so give your students the gift of knowing what to expect. "Hey, everyone, we have a substitute teacher in music today, so the schedule will be a little different." "Tomorrow we're having a fire drill around 10:30." "I'll be out on Thursday, but Mrs. Rodriguez will be here, and she's amazing." These heads-up announcements can prevent huge meltdowns for kids whose traumas have taught them that change equals danger.

- **Throw out the labels:** That folder from last year with the "Behavioral concerns" or "Difficult student" label? Toss it. Or at least put it away and commit to seeing this child with fresh eyes. Kids live up (or down) according to our expectations, and those labels become self-fulfilling prophecies faster than you can say "office referral." Give every child a clean slate. Yes, even the one who drove you crazy last semester.

- **Pause before responding:** When challenging behavior happens, give yourself three seconds before responding. Three seconds to breathe. Three seconds to remember that this child is communicating a critical message. Three seconds to choose curiosity over judgment. It's amazing how those three seconds can change what comes next.

- **Start an observation log:** You don't need a fancy app or journal, just a small notebook or your phone. When challenging behavior happens, jot down:
    - ▸ Time of day
    - ▸ What was happening right before
    - ▸ What the behavior looked like
    - ▸ What was happening in the child's life (if you know)

    You'll be surprised at the patterns that emerge. Maybe meltdowns always happen right before lunch (blood sugar!). Maybe shutdowns occur every Monday (tough weekends at home). Maybe arguments spike during transition times (change is hard for children affected by trauma).

A BLUEPRINT FOR FULL IMPLEMENTATION

Ready to go deeper? Designing a truly trauma-responsive classroom requires systematic change over time. We're not talking about quick fixes or surface-level adjustments, but about fundamentally shifting how you understand and respond to student behavior. Here's your roadmap for creating a classroom where every child feels seen, understood, and supported.

STEP 1: Learn about trauma basics.

You can't respond to trauma if you don't understand it. The good news is that you've already started to understand it by reading this book! Keep learning about how trauma affects developing brains, what trauma responses look like, and why traditional discipline doesn't work for children affected by trauma.

A valuable resource is the book *The Body Keeps the Score* by Bessel van der Kolk. It dives into the research behind how trauma literally rewires the developing brain. (Warning: it's heavy but brilliant and will give you a whole new understanding of why traditional discipline fails.) A second suggestion is online training from the National Child Traumatic Stress Network for practical, classroom-focused strategies you can implement immediately.

STEP 2: **Observe during calm periods.**

Calm periods are where the detective work begins. When students are regulated and calm, watch for their baseline behaviors. How do they usually interact with peers? What's their typical energy level? How do they usually respond to transitions?

This calm behavior becomes your comparison point. When you notice a student is "off" or more withdrawn, hyper, or argumentative than usual, that's your cue that a challenge is occurring in the student's world.

STEP 3: **Look for patterns in behavior triggers.**

Keep that observation log we previously discussed, but now get more specific. Look for:

- **Time patterns:** Are challenging behaviors more likely to occur in the morning? After lunch? End of day?

- **Activity patterns:** Do problems arise during independent work? Group activities? Transitions?

- **Social patterns:** Are issues more common around certain peers? After social conflicts?

- **Calendar patterns:** Are Mondays harder? Days after breaks? Around holidays?

One teacher discovered that her "defiant" student only had problems on days when he rode the bus to school. Turns out, he was being bothered by older children on the bus and arrived at school already dysregulated. The teacher came up with a simple solution by creating a special morning routine where he could come straight to the classroom to help set up, which gave him time to decompress from the bus ride and feel important.

STEP 4: Keep notes (trust us on this one).

Your brain is amazing, but it's not a computer. You won't remember patterns without documentation. Keep notes about what you observe, what you try, and what works (or doesn't). This documentation serves multiple purposes:

- It helps you see patterns you'd otherwise miss.
- It shows growth over time (for both you and the students).
- It provides evidence if and when you need to advocate for additional support.
- It helps you remember what strategies work best.

STEP 5: Develop individualized response strategies.

Once you understand a student's patterns and triggers, you can develop personalized strategies to minimize them. This customization involves helping each child find a workable way to access the same learning environment.

Perhaps the student who melts down during transitions gets a two-minute warning. Maybe the child who argues when feeling powerless gets choices about how to complete tasks. And the kid who shuts down when overwhelmed can go to a quiet corner to regroup.

These aren't accommodations; they're success strategies.

OVERCOMING PUSHBACK

When you start responding to behavior differently, colleagues, administrators, and parents may question your approach. Their response is normal. Trauma-responsive practices challenge deeply held beliefs about discipline and classroom management. Here's how to address the most common concerns while staying committed to seeing behavior as communication rather than defiance.

I don't have time for all this touchy-feely stuff. In reality, you don't have time *not* to do this. Think about the amount of time you currently spend on behavior management—writing referrals, calling parents, dealing with meltdowns, and reteaching after disruptions. This approach prevents most of those issues before they start. One teacher tracked her time for a month and found she was spending an average of forty-five minutes per day on behavior-related interruptions. After implementing trauma-responsive strategies, that number dropped to about ten minutes per day. That's thirty-five extra minutes of teaching time.

Our school has zero-tolerance policies. Work within the system while advocating for change. You can still implement trauma-responsive practices while following school policies. Document the details, show administrators the positive results, and gradually build support for systemic change. Most administrators are concerned about reducing office referrals and improving the school climate. When you can show that your approach achieves these goals better than traditional discipline, you'll have allies.

You're letting them get away with it. This comment is probably the most common pushback, and it comes from a fundamental misunderstanding of what accountability looks like. There's a huge difference between consequences and punishment. Punishment is what we do *to* children to make them suffer for their behavior. Consequences are chances for learning and growth that naturally follow from choices. We're teaching students valuable lessons about accountability when we help them understand why they acted the way they did and develop better strategies for next time, support them in making amends if they've hurt someone, and teach them regulation skills so they can make different choices. Punishing trauma responses retraumatizes kids and confirms their beliefs that they can't trust adults.

My colleagues keep giving me unsolicited advice about being too soft. Ah, the hallway critics. Every school has them. Here are a few responses that shut down unhelpful commentary while staying professional:

- "I appreciate your concern. I'm seeing great results with this approach."

- "Every child is different. This process is working for this particular student."

- "I'd rather err on the side of compassion than punishment."

- "My focus is on teaching replacement behaviors, not just stopping unwanted ones."

If the criticism persists, loop in your administrator. A message such as, "I wanted to let you know about the success I'm having with trauma-responsive approaches. Here's the data ..." can provide cover and build support.

THE HACK IN ACTION

Let's see what this looks like in real classrooms.

Kindergartner DeShawn had frequent meltdowns—screaming, throwing things, and sometimes hitting. Traditional consequences weren't working, and everyone was at their wits' end. His teacher, Ms. Rosales, noticed that DeShawn's meltdowns often happened during transitions or when routines changed. She also learned that DeShawn had recently moved in with his grandmother after his mother entered rehab.

Ms. Rosales started giving DeShawn extra warnings about transitions: "In five minutes, we'll clean up and go to lunch." She created a visual schedule he could follow and gave him special jobs during transition times. Most importantly, she taught him words for his big feelings: "It sounds like you're feeling frustrated. Let's take some deep breaths together."

The result? DeShawn's meltdowns decreased by 90 percent. He learned to use his words instead of his fists. Ms. Rosales discovered that underneath the behavior problems was a scared little boy who needed extra support during a difficult time in his life.

Third-grader Anton couldn't stay in his seat. Every few minutes, he'd pop up, wander around, or find an excuse to sharpen his pencil. His teacher, Ms. Chen, tried everything: behavior charts, losing recess, and moving his desk closer to hers. Nothing worked. Anton kept getting in trouble, and Ms. Chen kept getting frustrated. She started observing patterns. She noticed Anton's wandering increased when he was anxious or when the classroom felt too stimulating. Instead of trying to make him sit still, she gave him movement jobs: collecting papers, watering plants, and cleaning the whiteboard. She also discovered that Anton focused better when he had something to fidget with, so she provided stress balls and fidget tools for the whole class (because movement helps many kids, not just Anton, and it didn't single him out).

The result? Anton got his movement needs met without disrupting the learning. His academic performance improved because he could focus. Ms. Chen stopped feeling like she was constantly battling him. Win-win-win.

Seventh-grader Jasmine seemed to argue about everything. "Why do we have to do this?" "This is stupid." "I already know this." Her teachers were exhausted from the constant power struggles and started giving her detentions for "disrespectful attitude."

Instead of taking the bait, Jasmine's English teacher, Mr. Wilson, got curious. He noticed that Jasmine's argumentative behavior increased when she felt confused or overwhelmed. He realized she was using arguments to avoid tasks that felt too challenging.

Mr. Wilson started approaching Jasmine's resistance differently: "It sounds like this assignment feels overwhelming. What part is tricky for you?" or "I hear that you're frustrated. Let's figure out how to make this work better for you."

The result? Once Jasmine felt heard instead of judged, the arguments decreased dramatically. She started asking for help instead of picking fights. Her grades improved, and Mr. Wilson began to enjoy having her in class.

When we shift from reacting to behavior to responding to communication, the entire situation changes. We stop seeing problem students and start seeing children with problems. We stop asking, "How do I make this behavior stop?" and start asking, "What does this child need from me right now?"

This practice is about becoming the kind of adult every child deserves: one who sees beyond the behavior to the human being underneath.

The most powerful tool in your toolkit isn't a behavior chart or a consequence ladder; it's your relationship with each student. When children feel seen, understood, and valued, most behavioral problems tend to resolve themselves. When they feel safe with you, they can access the part of their brain that is open to learning, growing, and making good choices.

You might be the only safe adult in a child's life. You might be the only person who sees the student's pain as communication rather than defiance. Every child who enters your classroom is doing the best they can with what they have. Your job isn't to judge whether each student's best is good enough; your job is to help them expand what's possible.

When we reframe behavior as communication and respond with curiosity instead of judgment, we are changing the school climate, and we are changing lives. And isn't that why we became teachers in the first place?

REFLECTION
QUESTIONS

1. **What patterns do you notice in your most challenging students?** Think beyond the obvious behaviors to the triggers, timing, and context.

2. **How are you contributing to behavior challenges?** This isn't about blame; it's about recognizing where minor adjustments in your approach might yield major results.

3. **What would change if you viewed every behavior as communication?** How might it shift your responses in challenging moments?

4. **Which students are carrying the heaviest backpacks?** What do you know about their lives outside of school that might inform your responses to their behaviors?

5. **How can you build stronger relationships during calm moments?** What opportunities for connection exist in your daily routine?

Remember, you don't have to be perfect at this. You have to be willing to see your students' behaviors as their best attempts to communicate important messages to you. Your willingness to *truly listen* is where transformation begins.

HACK 2

FOCUS ON STRENGTHS, NOT DEFICITS

Build Resilience Through Strengths-Based Approaches

*There needs to be a lot more emphasis on what
a child can do instead of what he cannot do.*
— TEMPLE GRANDIN, ETHOLOGIST AND AUTISM ADVOCATE

THE INDIVIDUALIZED EDUCATION program meeting was going as expected. Twelve adults sat around a conference table, each armed with folders thick with documentation about what ten-year-old MJ couldn't do. "Struggles with reading comprehension." "Below grade level in math." "Difficulty with peer interactions." "Challenges with executive functioning." His mother sat quietly, shrinking in her seat with each deficit that was added to the official record.

Then, the IEP meeting took an unexpected turn. Ms. O'Neale, MJ's art teacher, cleared her throat. "I'd like to add something," she said, opening a new folder. "MJ sees the world differently than other kids, and that's actually his superpower. Last week, he noticed that our class turtle looked sad and suggested we rearrange the habitat to face the window. He was right; she became much more active. He also taught three other students how to shade with charcoal because he had figured out a technique I'd never seen before."

The room went quiet. MJ's mom looked up for the first time in twenty minutes, tears in her eyes. "Really?" she whispered.

"Really," Ms. O'Neale continued. "MJ has an incredible ability to notice details others miss. He thinks outside the box naturally. He's also one of the most empathetic kids I've ever taught. Yes, he struggles with some academic areas, but he has strengths that many adults would envy."

Later that day, MJ's mom sat with him at their kitchen table, tears still in her eyes. "Your art teacher said something today that you need to hear," she began, and then she shared every word Ms. O'Neale had spoken about his unique gifts. For the first time in his school career, MJ learned that someone had focused on what he could do rather than on what he couldn't. Someone had seen his differences as assets rather than deficits.

That moment changed MJ's world, both in how the school team approached his education and in how he saw himself.

THE PROBLEM: WE'VE BECOME DEFICIT DETECTIVES

Our educational system has been obsessed with what's wrong. Walk into any school building, and you'll find file cabinets and digital files stuffed with deficit documentation. Teachers can be known for documenting more areas of concern than paranoid security guards do. We've become archaeological experts at digging up all the tasks children can't do while completely missing the treasures of what they can.

This process is especially devastating for students impacted by trauma, who often arrive at school already carrying messages about their inadequacy. Trauma whispers lies like, "You're not enough," "You can't do anything right," and "There's something wrong with you." When we use deficit-focused approaches with these children, we're essentially handing their trauma a megaphone.

Every time we lead with what's lacking, we're confirming trauma's narrative. Every deficit-focused conversation becomes evidence that the students are, indeed, broken. Every intervention designed to "fix" them reinforces the belief that they need fixing in the first place.

But here's what's extra troubling about this approach: a deficit obsession doesn't only damage kids affected by trauma; it hurts all our students. When we consistently focus on gaps, weaknesses, and areas of need, we accidentally teach children that their identity is defined by what they lack rather than by what they possess. We create perfection-seeking humans who are terrified of making mistakes because mistakes become evidence of their inadequacy.

Let's talk about the sneaky ways deficit thinking shows up in our everyday language. "She's a non-reader." Wait, what? Is she unable to read at all, or does she read below grade level? "He has no friends." Really? Or does he have one good friend instead of a large social circle? "She can't do math." Hold up. Can she not count to five, or does she struggle with basic fact fluency?

These labels become identity statements. When we say a child can't do something, the student internalizes that message as a reflection of their identity rather than where they are in their learning journey. We've turned temporary learning states into permanent identity badges. Nobody wants to be the kid wearing the "needs improvement" jersey for life.

Here's another uncomfortable truth about deficit thinking: it's often culturally biased. When a middle-class white student questions authority or thinks outside the box, some teachers with the same race, ethnicity, or cultural experience might call those students creative or independent. But when a student from a different cultural background exhibits the same behaviors, those teachers might be more likely to label the student as defiant or non-compliant. Deficit thinking doesn't exist in a vacuum; it's shaped by our unconscious biases about what "good" students look like.

The education system has also created a bizarre situation where children's strengths get ignored if they don't align with traditional academic markers. The kid who can fix anything with his hands gets labeled "not college material." The student who can mediate peer conflicts gets seen as "too social." The child who asks thoughtful questions gets marked down for "being off-task." We're punishing kids for having abilities that don't fit into our narrow definition of school success. It's like we've decided that there's only one flavor of smart, and if you're not that particular flavor, then you're plain and overlooked.

And let's be honest about another fact: deficit thinking is exhausting for educators, and it's especially exhausting for our students. When an entire school experience revolves around what one can't do, then where's the motivation to keep trying? When every conversation focuses on the weaknesses, then where's the inspiration to grow? When an identity becomes synonymous with one's struggles, then where's the hope that the situation will get better?

A deficit approach is causing teachers to burn out at an alarming rate. When your job becomes a constant battle to fix what's "wrong" with kids, when your success is measured only by test scores that highlight deficits, and when every meeting focuses on problems rather than possibilities, then teaching stops being joyful. We entered education to inspire and empower, not to catalog inadequacies. Yet, our deficit-focused system has turned many passionate educators into weary warriors fighting battles they can never win.

The impact on teacher morale is devastating. When we're constantly swimming against the tide of what students can't do, we start believing that we can't make a difference. We begin to see ourselves through the same deficit lens that we apply to our students. "I can't reach these kids." "I'm not good at classroom management." "I'm failing as a teacher." The system that teaches us to focus on student deficits inevitably makes us hyper-aware of our own perceived inadequacies.

But here's what's deeply flawed about this approach that has historically been the focus of our entire educational system. From the moment children enter school, we're assessing what they don't know and trying to fill those gaps. Kindergarten readiness checklists focus on what skills children lack. Standardized tests highlight where students fall short. Report cards emphasize areas needing improvement. Professional development centers on addressing student deficiencies. Even our special education system, while well-intentioned, is built on documenting what children cannot do.

We've created a massive institutional machine that primarily functions to identify holes in children's knowledge and abilities. Our assessment systems, curriculum frameworks, intervention programs, and accountability measures all reinforce the same message: to find what's missing and fix it. We've become so skilled at deficit detection that we've forgotten how to recognize assets.

A systemic focus on gaps isn't accidental; it's embedded in the structure of how we think about education. We call it "diagnostic teaching," as if our students are patients with diseases to be cured. We talk about "achievement gaps" and "learning deficits," as if children are broken vessels with cracks to be sealed. We design "remediation" programs as if learning differences are illnesses requiring treatment.

Consider how our grading systems work. An "A" means you got everything right; anything less means you got something wrong. We don't have grades that celebrate creativity, persistence, growth, or unique thinking. We don't assess students' abilities to ask thoughtful questions, support their peers, or see problems from fresh perspectives. Our entire evaluation structure is designed to identify and penalize what students don't know rather than celebrate and build on what they do.

The testing industry has made this even worse. When schools' funding, teachers' evaluations, and administrators' jobs depend on test scores, the pressure to focus on deficits becomes overwhelming. Schools spend months preparing for tests that measure a narrow slice of human intelligence while ignoring the vast array of capabilities students possess. We teach to the test, intervene based on test results, and judge our success by test outcomes. The message is clear: only certain types of intelligence matter, and if you don't have those, you're deficient.

> **EVERY CHILD WHO WALKS INTO OUR CLASSROOM HAS STRENGTHS, TALENTS, INTERESTS, AND CAPABILITIES.**

Traditional teacher preparation programs often perpetuate this thinking. While some innovative programs emphasize strengths-based approaches, too many future educators still learn primarily about learning disabilities, behavior disorders, and achievement gaps without adequate focus on multiple intelligences, cultural assets, or strengths-based pedagogy. Too often, we train teachers to be problem-finders rather than strength-builders, teaching them to focus on deficits and create remediation plans without equally emphasizing how to identify and nurture the unique gifts every child possesses.

The professional development offered to practicing teachers often reinforces the same patterns. Sessions focus on closing achievement gaps, addressing learning deficits, and managing challenging behaviors. Rarely do we see workshops on discovering hidden strengths, building on cultural assets, or using student interests to accelerate learning. The message teachers receive is that their job is to fix what's broken rather than cultivate what's possible.

But a tragic part of deficit thinking is that it's completely unnecessary. Every child who walks into our classroom has strengths, talents, interests, and capabilities. Every one. Yes, even the kid who drives you up the wall. Yes, even the student who struggles with all subjects. Yes, even the child whose behaviors challenge every ounce of your patience and creativity.

The problem isn't that our students lack strengths. The problem is that we've been trained to look for problems instead of possibilities. We've created a system that's remarkably efficient at identifying what children can't do while ignoring what they can do. We've become deficit detectives when we should be strength explorers.

THE HACK: FOCUS ON STRENGTHS, NOT DEFICITS

So, what's the alternative? It starts with a revolutionary shift in perspective. Instead of asking, "What's wrong with this child?" we can ask, "What's strong with this child?" Instead of, "What needs to be fixed?" we can wonder, "What needs to be fed?" This Hack is about starting from a place of abundance rather than scarcity.

This approach works because it aligns with how human beings develop and thrive. People perform better, persist longer, and achieve more when they operate from their strengths rather than constantly trying to fix their weaknesses. When we focus on what students can do, we boost their confidence, engagement, and willingness to tackle challenges.

Strengths-based teaching is particularly powerful for students who may have experienced trauma because it directly counters the negative messages they've internalized. Instead of confirming their fears about being broken or inadequate, we can help them discover capabilities they didn't know they had. This shift in self-perception can be life-changing.

Understand What Strengths Look Like

Before we can enhance students' strengths, we need to expand our definition of strengths. Most educators have been trained to recognize a narrow range of abilities, such as reading above grade level, following directions perfectly, sitting quietly, and scoring well on tests. But human intelligence is far more diverse and complex than traditional academic measures suggest.

Strengths can be cognitive, such as seeing patterns that others miss, asking questions that change the direction of discussions, or finding creative solutions to problems. They can be social-emotional, like naturally including others, mediating conflicts with wisdom beyond their years, or bringing humor to tense situations. They can be kinesthetic, like learning through movement, possessing incredible fine motor skills, or understanding concepts better when they can manipulate objects.

Sometimes, strengths hide behind behaviors that annoy us. The student who argues about everything might have exceptional critical-thinking skills and the intellectual courage to voice unpopular opinions. The child who can't sit still might have incredible kinesthetic intelligence that we're trying to suppress. The kid who talks too much might be a natural communicator with strong verbal processing abilities.

Cultural and linguistic strengths are often overlooked entirely. The student who speaks multiple languages brings cognitive flexibility and global perspectives. The child whose family has taught them to question authority appropriately brings critical-thinking skills that we should celebrate, not suppress. The student whose culture emphasizes community and collaboration brings social intelligence that traditional individualistic academic settings often miss. (For more ideas about how to integrate student culture and language to create rich learning experiences for all students, see the book *Hacking Culturally Inclusive Teaching* by Kendra Nalubega-Booker.)

Survival skills that students developed through adversity are among the most underrecognized strengths. Whether shaped by instability, loss, or trauma, these experiences can forge remarkable capacities. The student who's learned to read adults' emotions for safety has incredible emotional intelligence. The child who's had to care for siblings has developed advanced responsibility and nurturing abilities. The kid who's moved frequently has learned adaptability and resilience that many adults lack.

Children who have been in the foster care system, in particular, often develop remarkable strengths that schools completely overlook. A child who's lived in multiple placements has learned to assess new environments quickly, adapt to different family systems, and form connections despite uncertainty. The child has developed survival skills, emotional regulation strategies, and resilience that would be considered advanced in any adult. Yet, instead of recognizing these qualities as incredible life skills, educators often focus only on the student's deficits in traditional academics or behavioral challenges that are normal responses to trauma and instability.

The Core Strategy: Become a Strength Detective

Your new job is to become a detective, but instead of looking for problems, you're hunting for assets. Every child has them, but some are more hidden than others. Your mission is to discover each child's assets, name them, celebrate them, and use them as bridges to new learning.

This mission means fundamentally changing how you observe and interact with students. Instead of noticing what they're not doing, start paying attention to what they are doing. Instead of focusing on where they fall short, focus on where they shine. Instead of seeing behaviors as problems to solve, see them as potential strengths to redirect.

SURVIVAL SKILLS THAT STUDENTS DEVELOPED THROUGH ADVERSITY ARE AMONG THE MOST UNDERRECOGNIZED STRENGTHS.

Start by expanding your observation lens. Watch students during unstructured time to see what they naturally gravitate toward. Notice how they interact with peers, what topics spark their curiosity, and what activities make them lose track of time. Pay attention to the questions they ask, the connections they make, and the unique perspectives they bring to discussions.

Look for patterns in their engagement. Some students come alive during hands-on activities, while others prefer abstract discussions. Some need time to process internally, while others think out loud. Some work best alone, while others thrive in collaborative settings. None of these preferences are learning deficits; they're valuable information about how each child learns most effectively.

Use Strengths as Learning Bridges

Once you've identified students' strengths, the real magic happens when you use those strengths to support learning in other areas. Personalizing instruction does not involve watering down content or avoiding challenging material. This process is about creating multiple pathways to the same learning destination. Think of strengths as the bridge that helps students cross from "I can't do this" to "I can tackle this challenge."

Academic Bridges: Connect Interests to Curriculum

The key is to find authentic connections between what students love and what they need to learn. It requires creativity, and the payoff is enormous when students realize their passions have value in academic settings.

For elementary students, their interests become powerful entry points to literacy and numeracy. The kindergartner obsessed with trucks can practice sorting with toy vehicles, learn letter sounds through transportation words, and develop writing skills by creating construction site stories. The second-grader who knows every dinosaur name can tackle challenging vocabulary through paleontology texts and practice measurement by comparing fossil sizes.

Middle schoolers can bridge developing interests to sophisticated academic skills. The student who's passionate about K-pop can analyze lyrics for literary devices, research Korean culture for social studies, and explore the mathematics behind music production. The aspiring baker can use cooking to understand fractions in math, study nutrition science, and practice procedural writing through recipes.

High school students can leverage their strengths for college preparation. The natural leader can analyze political speeches for rhetorical strategies and develop presentation skills through debates. The visual artist can explore geometry through perspective drawing and the study of color theory in chemistry.

Social-Emotional Bridges: Use Strengths to Build Relationships and Regulation

Some students' greatest strengths lie in their social-emotional intelligence, and these abilities can become bridges to academic success when channeled appropriately. The naturally empathetic student can become a peer mediator while developing communication skills and might excel at character analysis in literature because they intuitively understand human motivations.

The class comedian has verbal intelligence that can be channeled into creative writing or drama performances. Instead of constantly redirecting their jokes, give them appropriate outlets: let them write funny story endings, create comic strips that demonstrate science concepts, or develop entertaining research presentations.

Children who have been in the foster care system often develop exceptional abilities to read social situations and adapt to new environments. These skills can be incredible assets in group projects and peer tutoring situations. The student who's learned to quickly assess new families has developed observational skills that transfer to scientific inquiry and character analysis in literature.

Behavioral Bridges: Channel "Problem" Behaviors into Strengths

Many behaviors that frustrate teachers are strengths in disguise, waiting for appropriate outlets and redirection.

The argumentative student is likely to possess strong critical-thinking skills. Instead of silencing the student's challenges, assign the student to be the official devil's advocate in discussions or to research controversial topics. The young person's natural inclination to challenge ideas becomes an academic asset.

The student who struggles to sit still has kinesthetic intelligence that needs movement to support learning. Let the child stand while working, use manipulatives for math concepts, or act out historical events. The student's need for movement becomes a learning strategy rather than a behavioral problem.

The bossy student often has natural leadership abilities that need appropriate channels. Put this child in charge of group projects or as a peer mentor. Teach students the difference between leadership and dominance, and don't crush their natural inclination to organize.

The student who talks too much is often a verbal processor with strong communication skills. Give this student chances to think out loud through peer discussions or oral presentations. The verbal processing becomes a learning strategy for tackling complex content.

Build Strength Recognition into Daily Practice

Strengths-based teaching isn't an occasional practice; it becomes woven into the fabric of daily classroom life. It influences how you speak to students, design lessons, assess learning, and communicate with families.

Start with your language. Instead of "You need to work on your handwriting," try "Your ideas are so creative; let's find ways to help others see that creativity clearly." Instead of "You're behind in reading," say "You're a strong visual learner; let's use that to accelerate your reading growth." Small shifts in language create massive shifts in how students see themselves.

Design lessons that allow different students to shine at different times. If today's math lesson favors quick computational thinking, tomorrow's might emphasize visual-spatial reasoning or collaborative problem-solving. Create opportunities for students to teach each other, share expertise, and contribute their unique perspectives to class discussions.

The beauty of this approach is that it works across all educational environments. Whether you're in a traditional classroom, alternative setting, special education environment, or any other learning space, every student has strengths waiting to be discovered and developed. The key is learning to see them and use them as bridges to new learning.

When we implement strengths-based approaches systematically, we create classroom cultures where all students can thrive. We teach children that there are many ways to be smart, to contribute, and to forge a unique path to success. Such strengths-based perspectives prepare them for academic achievement and lifelong resilience and confidence.

WHAT **YOU** CAN DO TOMORROW

Ready to shift from deficit detective to strengths explorer? Here are concrete actions you can implement immediately to transform how you see and support your students.

- **Identify one strength for each student, and share it personally.** Look at your class roster and write down one specific, observable strength for each student. Not generic compliments like "nice" (which tells us nothing), but specific assets like "excellent spatial reasoning" or "natural ability to make others feel included." Then share these strengths with each student individually. Many have never heard an adult name their capabilities before.

- **Reframe one problem behavior as a potential strength.** Consider a student whose behavior often frustrates others, and look at it through a different lens. The child who interrupts frequently might be eager to contribute and full of ideas. The kid who ignores instructions might have strong problem-solving skills. The overly cautious student might be a thoughtful decision-maker. The child who constantly questions everything might be naturally curious. Find appropriate outlets for these qualities instead of trying to eliminate them. Pro tip: When you give the class arguers official permission to argue, they often become your most thoughtful discussion leaders. It's like reverse psychology, but educational.

- **Use a student's interest or strength in an academic lesson.** Incorporate what you know about students' passions into your teaching. Use dragon and unicorn examples for the fantasy fan's math problems, character attributes for the gamer's data analysis, or song lyrics for the aspiring musician's reading comprehension. This shows students that their interests have value in academic settings.

- **Send home positive communication about students' strengths.** Most school-home communication focuses on problems. Flip that script by highlighting specific strengths you've observed. "Baker showed incredible problem-solving skills today," or "Sarah's creativity really shone through in her project." Parents start seeing their children through your eyes, and kids start believing they're capable learners.

- **Display student strengths and achievements prominently.** Create classroom displays that celebrate diverse types of intelligence and growth. Spotlight improvement, creativity, kindness, persistence, and unique thinking alongside traditional academic achievements. Make sure all students see themselves represented positively somewhere in your space.

- **Create one strength showcase opportunity.** Give one student a week the chance to teach classmates about an area of expertise. The video game expert can share problem-solving strategies, the zoo-loving student can teach about animal behavior, or the artist can demonstrate a painting technique. These showcases inspire confidence while creating authentic learning opportunities for everyone.

A BLUEPRINT FOR FULL IMPLEMENTATION

Building a comprehensive strengths-based classroom culture requires intentional planning and systematic implementation. Here's your roadmap for creating an environment where every student's assets are recognized, developed, and celebrated.

STEP 1: Become a strengths detective and create comprehensive student profiles.

Start by systematically observing each student to identify their unique combination of abilities, interests, and qualities. Include traditional academic skills and look beyond them to observe social-emotional strengths, character traits, cultural assets, creative abilities, and survival skills that children affected by trauma often develop. Create profiles that capture all of these skills plus the students' interests. Update these profiles regularly and share them with families and other educators.

STEP 2: Design learning experiences that tap into diverse strengths.

Use your knowledge of student strengths to create multiple pathways to the same learning objectives by planning lessons that include visual, auditory, and kinesthetic elements and offering chances for both independent and collaborative work. Allow students to demonstrate their learning in various ways. Connect academic content to student interests and real-world applications, and design activities where different students can shine at different times, ensuring everyone experiences success. Experiment with developing choice menus for assignments that honor different strengths while maintaining rigorous learning objectives. Instead of requiring all students to write traditional essays, offer options like creating infographics, recording podcasts, building models, or designing presentations.

STEP 3: Establish systems for recognizing and celebrating growth.

Create formal and informal ways to acknowledge different types of achievements and improvements. Implement weekly growth spotlights to highlight student progress, strength walls to display various talents and accomplishments, peer recognition systems where students nominate classmates, regular positive communication with families, and documentation that tracks growth over time rather than solely point-in-time achievement.

STEP 4: Teach students to identify and articulate their strengths.

Many students, especially those who've experienced trauma or academic struggles, need explicit instruction in recognizing their capabilities. Use regular reflection activities, create ways for students to share interests and talents, implement portfolio approaches that show growth over time, teach the language of multiple intelligences and diverse strengths, and help students connect their abilities to future goals and aspirations.

STEP 5: Share the strengths perspective with your educational community.

Become an advocate for asset-based approaches beyond your classroom. Start meetings and conversations by highlighting student strengths, model strengths-based language with colleagues, document and share positive outcomes, advocate for strengths-based approaches in IEP meetings and team discussions, and provide resources to colleagues interested in asset-based education.

OVERCOMING PUSHBACK

When you start focusing on strengths, some colleagues, administrators, and parents may question your approach. Here's how to address the most common concerns while staying true to your commitment to see students as capable.

But they really do have deficits that we need to address. Absolutely, and strengths-based approaches don't mean ignoring genuine learning needs. The difference is in how we approach those needs. Instead of starting with deficits and trying to fix them, we start with strengths and use them to address areas of growth. When we build on strengths, students make more progress in challenging areas than when we focus exclusively on weaknesses.

A positive focus isn't realistic; the real world is harsh. This objection assumes that criticism and a deficit focus prepare students for success, but research proves the opposite. People perform better and achieve more when they operate from their strengths. The most successful organizations now focus on employee assets rather than trying to eliminate weaknesses. More importantly, deficit-focused approaches often create learned helplessness, while strengths-based approaches develop resilience and a growth mindset.

This approach sounds like feel-good fluff that lowers expectations. Strengths-based teaching allows for higher expectations because students are more willing to tackle challenges when they feel capable and valued. This approach involves helping students access challenging material through their areas of strength and building confidence to persist through difficulties.

Other teachers focus on problems, so I should too. You have the chance to be an educator who sees each student differently and helps them discover capabilities they didn't know they had. You can't control other teachers' approaches, but you can model asset-based thinking and share the positive results you see. Often, colleagues become interested when they witness how much more engaged and successful students become under strengths-based approaches.

THE HACK IN ACTION

Let's follow Kenny, a sixth-grader who arrived at Mr. Bennett's classroom with a reputation that preceded him. Previous teachers had labeled him as "argumentative," "disrespectful," and "a student who constantly questions authority." Traditional approaches had focused on trying to shut down his challenges with consequences and compliance-based interventions, but these approaches didn't work.

Mr. Bennett decided to see Kenny through a different lens. Instead of viewing Kenny's questioning as a sign of disrespect, he recognized it as evidence of strong critical-thinking skills and intellectual courage. Rather than trying to silence Kenny's voice, he gave it appropriate and valued outlets.

The transformation began when Mr. Bennett officially appointed Kenny as the class devil's advocate during discussions, tasked with finding flaws in arguments and asking challenging questions. He gave Kenny research projects on controversial topics that required investigating multiple perspectives. When conflicts arose between classmates, Mr. Bennett used Kenny's natural leadership qualities by training him as a peer mediator.

Most importantly, Mr. Bennett reframed Kenny's questioning as intellectual curiosity rather than defiance. When Kenny challenged an idea, instead of responding with "Because I said so," Mr. Bennett engaged Kenny's critical thinking. "That's a thoughtful challenge. What evidence are you basing that perspective on?"

This approach honored Kenny's intelligence while teaching him how to express disagreement respectfully.

The results were remarkable. Kenny's "argumentative" behavior decreased dramatically once his critical thinking was valued rather than suppressed. His academic performance soared because he was intellectually engaged rather than fighting power struggles. Other students began seeing him as a thoughtful leader rather than a troublemaker.

By spring, Kenny was facilitating peer discussion groups and had been recommended for the school debate team. His parents reported that he was excited about learning for the first time in years. The same qualities that had been labeled as problems became his greatest academic assets once they were recognized and channeled appropriately.

When we shift from deficit thinking to strengths-based approaches, we don't just change how we see our students; we change how they see themselves. This transformation is particularly powerful for children affected by trauma, who often carry internalized messages about their inadequacy. By consistently focusing on capabilities rather than deficits, we are helping to rewrite those negative internal narratives and increase genuine confidence and resilience.

Strengths-based teaching doesn't ignore learning needs or avoid challenging content. It helps all children discover that they have something valuable to contribute and use those assets as bridges to new learning. When students believe in their capabilities, they become willing to take risks, persist through difficulties, and reach their full potential. The results reflect effective teaching and life-changing education.

REFLECTION
QUESTIONS

1. **What strengths do you see in your most challenging students that you might have previously overlooked?** Push yourself to look beyond traditional academic abilities to social-emotional intelligence, survival skills, cultural assets, and unique perspectives.

2. **How can you use one student's specific strength as a bridge to support learning in a challenging area?** Think about a particular student and create a concrete plan for connecting the student's assets to curriculum content.

3. **What messages are you sending students about their capabilities through your language, displays, and focus?** Consider whether your classroom environment and communication patterns reinforce deficit thinking or celebrate diverse forms of intelligence.

4. **Which students in your classroom might not know their strengths, and how can you help them recognize their assets?** These students often need recognition of their strengths the most and could benefit from this approach.

HACK 3

DITCH THE PUBLIC BEHAVIOR CHART

Dismantle Discipline Systems That Retraumatize

The way we talk to our children becomes their inner voices.
— PEGGY O'MARA, NATURAL FAMILY LIVING ADVOCATE

EIGHT-YEAR-OLD LENA STARED at the behavior chart prominently displayed by the classroom door. Her name sat firmly in red. Again. As her classmates lined up for lunch, she felt their eyes on her, some sympathetic, others quietly grateful it wasn't them. The chart was intended to encourage better choices, but all Lena felt was the familiar burn of shame spreading across her cheeks.

What her teacher didn't know was that Lena had spent the morning before school hiding in the bathroom while her parents screamed at each other in the kitchen. She arrived at school with her nervous system already activated, hypervigilant and struggling to concentrate. When she couldn't sit still during art, when she forgot to raise her hand during reading, when she accidentally knocked over her water bottle during science, each incident moved her card down another color.

By lunchtime, that red card was not only displaying her behavior but broadcasting her most vulnerable moments to everyone who walked past. For a child whose home life already felt out of control, the public behavior chart had become another indicator that she didn't have safety or dignity.

THE PROBLEM: WE'RE PUBLICLY SHAMING STUDENTS IN THE NAME OF ACCOUNTABILITY

We've created elaborate systems designed to track, display, and broadcast children's most challenging moments to anyone who enters our rooms. Behavior charts, clip charts, color-coded folders that go home, and desk moves that isolate struggling students are all in the name of accountability and motivation. But here's what we're doing: we're taking children's worst moments and making them public, turning their struggles into entertainment for peers, and creating systems that function more like billboards advertising student pain than tools for supporting growth.

These public tracking systems are particularly devastating for students affected by trauma, who often arrive at school carrying invisible wounds from experiences beyond their control. For these children, shame triggers their fight, flight, freeze, or fawn responses. Stress hormones interfere with memory formation and learning. When students worry about their behavior status being displayed, their brains are less capable of absorbing new information.

This situation is especially problematic for children who have been in the foster care system, who may have experienced multiple placement changes and disrupted attachments. When these children seek connection from the teacher, they are not seeking attention but trying to form the stable relationship that a developing brain desperately needs. Public behavior tracking can retraumatize these vulnerable students by recreating dynamics of shame and rejection.

Children are remarkably perceptive about social hierarchies, and public behavior systems teach them to judge classmates based on their worst moments. These systems also trap teachers in cycles of negative interaction with the children who need connection the most, relying on external motivation that actually undermines an intrinsic drive over time.

THINK ABOUT THE LAST TIME YOU HAD A TERRIBLE DAY. HOW WOULD YOU HAVE FELT IF YOUR WORKPLACE POSTED YOUR STRUGGLES ON A PUBLIC CHART FOR EVERYONE TO SEE?

Think about the last time you had a terrible day. Maybe you snapped at a colleague, forgot an essential deadline, or made a mistake that affected others. How would you have felt if your workplace posted your struggles on a public chart for everyone to see? You'd probably start looking for a new job or hide in the supply closet until the humiliation passed.

The prefrontal cortex, responsible for impulse control and emotional regulation, doesn't fully mature until around age twenty-five. Yet our behavior charts expect kindergartners to demonstrate the self-control of adults. When they inevitably fall short of these unrealistic expectations, we label them as problems rather than recognizing the developmental mismatch in our systems. It's like expecting a toddler to file taxes or asking a teenager to make rational decisions about curfew. Spoiler alert: it won't end well.

We've created a system where we're punishing children for having normal trauma responses, and we're reinforcing public shaming as an acceptable response to human struggle. At this rate, we'll be prescribing academic antibiotics and recommending educational surgery.

THE HACK: DITCH THE PUBLIC BEHAVIOR CHART

The solution is not to abandon all expectations or structure but to replace shame-based systems with dignity-preserving approaches that support student growth and regulation. When we shift from public tracking to private support, from external control to internal motivation, we create environments where students can learn from mistakes without losing their sense of worth.

This transformation requires us to reimagine what accountability looks like. True accountability is not about publicizing struggles but about helping students understand the impact of their choices, develop skills for handling challenges, and make amends when they have caused harm. It means building internal motivation rather than relying on external pressure.

The Core Strategy: Address Behaviors Privately, Never Publicly

One foundation of trauma-responsive behavior support is to protect student dignity by handling all behavior concerns through private conversations rather than public displays. Without ignoring problems or lowering expectations, we can respond to struggles in ways that preserve relationships and promote genuine learning.

When a student is having difficulty, approach the student individually rather than announcing the struggle to the class. Get down to the student's eye level, use a calm voice, and focus on understanding what they need rather than what they did wrong. "I notice you're having a hard time focusing today. What's going on? How can I help?" becomes more powerful than any public consequence.

This private approach allows you to address the real issues behind challenging behavior. Maybe the student didn't sleep well, forgot to eat breakfast, or is worried about an issue at home. When you handle concerns privately, you can respond to the need rather than the surface behavior.

For students with trauma histories, private responses communicate safety and respect. They signal that you see them as worthy of dignity, even in their difficult moments. This practice creates trust and connection, which are prerequisites for genuine behavior change.

Assume Positive Intent and Show Grace

Instead of interpreting challenging behavior as defiance or disrespect, start by assuming that students are doing their best with the skills and resources they have at their disposal. By doing so, educators are responding to struggles with curiosity instead of judgment.

The statement, "I can see that you're frustrated. Let's figure out what's making this hard for you," conveys care while maintaining expectations. Grace means offering students the same patience and understanding that we hope for in our difficult moments, recognizing that learning self-regulation is a process, not a one-time achievement.

Provide Choices Within Structure

One of the most powerful alternatives to public consequences is to offer students choices about how to handle their challenges. Asking, "Would you like to take a break in the quiet corner, or would you prefer to move to a different spot?" gives students agency while addressing the need for change.

Choice-based responses help students rebuild a sense of control, which is often damaged by traumatic experiences. When students feel they have some power in determining their response to difficulties, they are more likely to engage cooperatively rather than defensively.

The key is to offer genuine choices that you can live with, not pseudo-choices that manipulate students into compliance. "Do you want to calm down here or in the hall?" works when both options are truly acceptable to you. "Do you want to stop talking or go to the principal?" isn't a choice because no reasonable person would choose the principal's office. That's a threat disguised as a choice, and students see right through it.

Focus on Intrinsic Motivation Through Interest and Autonomy

Instead of relying on external rewards like chart privileges or public recognition, focus on inspiring internal motivation through student interests, meaningful learning experiences, and appropriate autonomy. When students are engaged in work that matters to them and feel capable of success, most behavior problems resolve naturally.

This process might incorporate student interests into academic content, offer choices in how to demonstrate learning, or create opportunities for students to share their expertise with classmates. The goal is to make learning intrinsically rewarding rather than dependent on external motivators.

For children affected by trauma, rebuilding intrinsic motivation is particularly valuable because external systems can trigger feelings of powerlessness and a loss of agency. When students discover they can be successful and valued for their authentic contributions, they develop a genuine investment in their learning community.

Use Restorative Practices for Genuine Accountability

When students make mistakes that affect others, focus on repair rather than punishment. Restorative practices help students understand the impact of their choices and take meaningful action to make things right, creating accountability rather than compliance.

This method might involve helping a student who interrupted the class have a conversation about how interruptions affect classmates' learning, having a student who was unkind to a peer find ways to rebuild that relationship, or arranging for a student who damaged materials to help with classroom maintenance. The focus is on understanding the impact of their actions and taking responsibility rather than experiencing punishment.

Restorative approaches are particularly healing for children affected by trauma because they emphasize repair and reconnection rather than isolation and shame. They teach that mistakes do not define you, but how you respond to mistakes does.

WHAT **YOU** CAN DO TOMORROW

Ready to begin dismantling public shaming systems while maintaining high expectations and a supportive structure? These immediate actions will help you develop a more dignified and effective approach to supporting student behavior and establishing a classroom community.

- **Remove behavior charts and public tracking systems.** Take down those clip charts, color-coded displays, and any other systems that broadcast student struggles. If you are required to track behavior data, do it privately in a way that protects student dignity.

- **Start sending positive communication home instead.** Replace those daily behavior reports with positive notes highlighting student strengths, growth, or contributions. "Vincent showed incredible persistence in math today," or "Kai was so kind to a new student during lunch."

- **Begin keeping private notes of positive moments for each child.** Use your phone's notes app, a small notebook, or a folder system to record positive observations about each student. One suggestion is to use a file folder for each child's name and to add sticky notes inside. This system allows you to quickly see which sticky notes remain empty, helping you identify which children still need to be observed. "Hassan asked a thoughtful question that changed our whole discussion," or "Aaliyah helped a struggling peer without being asked."

- **Practice addressing a behavior issue privately.** The next time a student struggles, resist the urge to address it publicly. Instead, approach the learner quietly, get down to the student's level, and have a private conversation about what's happening and what is needed.

- **Replace a punitive consequence with a restorative conversation.** When a student makes a mistake that affects others, focus on helping the student understand the impact and find ways to make it right rather than imposing an unrelated consequence.

- **Establish a calm corner or cozy space.** Create a spot in your room where students can go to regulate their emotions without shame or punishment. Make it comfortable and teach students that taking breaks is a sign of wisdom, not weakness.

A BLUEPRINT FOR FULL IMPLEMENTATION

Creating a truly trauma-responsive approach to behavior support requires a systematic change in how you structure expectations, respond to challenges, and build classroom community. This work does not involve becoming permissive or abandoning account-ability; it is about creating more effective, humane systems that support student growth and relationships.

STEP 1: Design collaborative classroom agreements.

Instead of posting rules that you've created and imposed, work with your students to develop agreements about how they want to treat each other and take care of the learning environment. This process inspires investment and ownership rather than compliance.

Begin with discussions about what makes students feel safe, respected, and excited to learn. Generate ideas together about how to handle conflicts, mistakes, and challenges. Frame agreements as commitments to each other rather than rules to follow. Initiate these conversations during the first week of school and revisit them regularly throughout the year as your classroom commu-nity evolves and grows.

For younger students, use concrete scenarios to guide discussions. "What should we do when someone is talking and we have an idea?" or "How can we help a friend who's feeling frustrated?" For older students, explore deeper questions about respect, responsibility, and community-building. "What does it look like when everyone feels valued in our classroom?" or "How do we handle disagreements in ways that strengthen rather than damage relationships?"

Use language that emphasizes collective responsibility. Instead of saying, "Don't talk when others are talking," try phrases like, "We listen to each other's ideas," or "Everyone's voice matters in our classroom." Instead of "No running in the hallway," consider "We move through our school in ways to keep ourselves safe."

Notice how the positive framing tells students what to do rather than what not to do.

Make the agreements visual and accessible. Create posters together, have students illustrate the agreements, or develop hand signals that represent your community values. Consider having students sign the posted agreements as a symbolic commitment to their classroom community, making their investment visible and meaningful. Elementary students might draw pictures showing what the agreements look like in action. Middle schoolers could create infographics or design posters. High school students might develop role-play scenarios or create digital presentations about classroom community values.

> DIGNITY-PRESERVING BEHAVIOR SUPPORT RELIES HEAVILY ON RELATIONSHIPS, SO YOU NEED INTENTIONAL SYSTEMS FOR CREATING AND MAINTAINING CONNECTIONS WITH EVERY STUDENT, ESPECIALLY THOSE WHO STRUGGLE.

When challenges arise, refer back to these agreements as guides for problem-solving rather than rules that have been broken. "I notice we're struggling with our agreement about listening to each other. What's making this hard right now, and how can we support each other better?" This approach treats agreements as tools for growth rather than weapons for punishment.

Your classroom agreements can become living documents that you revisit regularly and adjust based on what's working and what needs attention. Schedule monthly or quarterly community meetings where students can suggest modifications, celebrate successes, and problem-solve ongoing challenges. But be willing to revisit them more often, as needed. When students help create the expectations, they are more likely to uphold the agreements and help each other meet them. More importantly, they develop investment in the classroom community rather than solely compliance with adult-imposed rules.

STEP 2: Develop proactive relationship-building systems.

Dignity-preserving behavior support relies heavily on relationships, so you need intentional systems for creating and maintaining connections with every student, especially those who struggle with traditional approaches.

Create daily connection rituals that allow you to check in with each student personally. This process might include greeting students individually at the door with specific, genuine comments about their interests, accomplishments, or observations. "Good morning, Ravi! How did your debate tournament go yesterday?" or "Hi, Suzy! I notice you brought that book you've been talking about." These brief moments signal that you see each student as an individual rather than another kid at a desk.

For students who arrive early or stay late, use transition times for informal conversations. Ask about their pets, weekend plans, favorite shows, or family traditions. Keep a small notebook or phone app where you jot down details students share so you can follow up later. "How's your grandmother feeling?" or "Did you finish that art project you were working on?" shows students that their lives matter to you beyond academics.

Implement regular class meetings or community circles where students can share successes, challenges, and appreciations. Structure these gatherings with consistent formats that feel safe and predictable. Elementary students might use a talking stick or a special chair. Middle schoolers could use journal prompts or discussion stems. High school students might prefer small-group check-ins before whole-class sharing. These gatherings foster a sense of community while giving you insights into students' lives and concerns. They also provide safe spaces for addressing conflicts and celebrating growth without singling anyone out negatively.

Establish private check-in systems for students who need extra support, possibly including brief morning conversations before class, signal systems that allow students to communicate their needs without words, or scheduled weekly meetings to discuss goals and strategies. Some students benefit from written check-ins through journals or note exchanges. Others prefer quick verbal check-ins during independent work time. The key is to build relationships *proactively* rather than waiting for problems to arise.

Create special jobs or responsibilities that provide natural openings for one-on-one interactions. The student who struggles with peer relationships might be your special messenger. The child who has difficulty with transitions could be in charge of warning other students about schedule changes. The student who needs movement might be responsible for distributing materials or organizing supplies. These roles provide positive attention while meeting individual needs.

Document positive interactions and growth for each student. Keep records of strengths you observe, interests they share, and progress they make. This documentation might be as simple as a notebook with a page for each student or a digital document with ongoing observations. "Lucia helped a struggling peer without being asked," "Jin showed incredible persistence with a challenging math problem," or "Carlos shared thoughtful insights about character motivation in our book." Such information becomes invaluable for understanding patterns, communicating with families, and advocating for students when challenges arise.

STEP 3: **Build regulation and social-emotional learning into daily practice.**

Rather than responding to dysregulation after it occurs, embed regulation support and social-emotional skill-building throughout your daily routines and academic instruction. Start each day with brief regulation activities that help students transition into learning mode. Such activities might include breathing exercises. Younger children can try the "smell the flower, blow out the candle" technique, and older children can try box breathing, with an inhale, hold, exhale, and hold for an equal number of counts. Movement activities could involve basic stretches, yoga poses, or energizing exercises that help students arrive in their bodies and brains. Mindfulness practices might include brief guided meditations, gratitude sharing, or a moment of quiet reflection.

Make these activities routine and optional, allowing students to participate in ways that feel comfortable while normalizing the attention on emotional well-being. Some students might need to observe before participating, and others might prefer to do their own versions of the activity. The goal is to create a classroom culture where emotional awareness and regulation are valued parts of learning.

Teach emotional literacy explicitly by helping students identify and name their feelings throughout the day. Create vocabularies of emotion words that go beyond happy, sad, mad, and scared. Use tools like feeling wheels, mood thermometers, or check-in systems that help students build nuanced awareness of their inner states. Model your emotional self-awareness through think-alouds, such as, "I notice I'm feeling overwhelmed right now, so I'm going to take three deep breaths before we continue." This approach of naming emotions teaches students that all states are valid and manageable. Incorporate a range of descriptive language in your interactions: "You seem frustrated with this writing assignment. What would help you feel more confident?" or "I can tell you're excited about this science experiment by the look on your face!" This steady use of affective vocabulary helps students develop the language they need to communicate their internal experiences rather than acting them out behaviorally.

Provide visual supports like feeling charts, regulation tools, and calm-down strategies displayed in accessible locations. Create regulation toolkits with items like stress balls, fidgets, breathing prompts, or calming images that students can access independently. Teach students about their nervous systems using age-appropriate language and help them understand that big emotions are normal and manageable.

Integrate social skills instruction into academic activities rather than treating it as a separate curriculum. Use literature to discuss character emotions and motivations, helping students practice perspective-taking and empathy. "Why do you think this character made that choice? How might the character be feeling?" Incorporate collaborative problem-solving into math and science activities so students must communicate, compromise, and work together toward common goals.

Provide opportunities for students to practice communication skills through presentations, discussions, and peer feedback activities. Teach sentence stems for disagreeing respectfully, asking for help, or giving compliments. "I see it differently because ..." or "That's an interesting point, and I would add ..." or "I need help understanding ..." give students a language for navigating social interactions successfully.

Create predictable routines for handling strong emotions when they arise. Teach students about their nervous systems using analogies like the "upstairs brain" (the prefrontal cortex—the thinking, problem-solving part) and "downstairs brain" (the brain stem and limbic system—the emotional, survival-focused part), helping students recognize when their "downstairs brain" has taken over and they need to help their "upstairs brain" get back in charge. Or use "zones" concepts like green zone (calm and ready to learn), yellow zone (starting to feel overwhelmed), and red zone (big emotions that make learning hard) to help students identify their emotional states. Help students recognize their personal warning signs of escalating emotions and develop regulation plans they can use on their own.

Offer multiple options for calming down, such as quiet corners with soft seating, sensory tools, breathing prompt cards, and movement breaks. Normalize the need for emotional breaks by saying things like, "It looks like your brain needs a reset. What would help you feel ready to learn again?" This language frames regulation breaks as wise choices rather than consequences or failures.

STEP 4: Establish restorative practices as your default response.

When conflicts or mistakes occur, make restorative practices your go-to approach rather than punitive consequences. Doing so requires shifting your mindset from "What consequence will prevent this behavior?" to "How can we repair harm and prevent future problems?"

Develop a simple process for addressing conflicts that focuses on understanding the impact and making amends. This process might include helping students identify what happened, how people were affected, what needs weren't met, and how to make things right. Teach students this process so they can use it independently.

Create opportunities for students to contribute positively to the classroom community when they've made mistakes. Instead of removing privileges or imposing unrelated consequences, help students find ways to help, contribute, or make amends that connect logically to their previous actions.

Establish regular restorative circles or meetings where the class can address ongoing issues, celebrate successes, and problem-solve challenges together. These gatherings grow a sense of community while teaching students that conflicts are normal parts of relationships that can be resolved through communication and mutual respect.

Teach students conflict resolution skills so they can handle peer disagreements independently, such as mediation processes, communication strategies, and problem-solving techniques that empower students to address issues without always needing adult intervention. Even the youngest students can start to learn these skills through role-playing and practice.

STEP 5: Create systems for ongoing communication and advocacy.

Because many families and administrators expect traditional behavior management systems, you'll want to proactively communicate your humanizing approach and the research that supports it. Develop clear explanations that emphasize outcomes rather than just philosophical principles. Prepare simple handouts, presentations, or short videos that describe what families and administrators can expect to see, how you will handle challenges, and why these approaches are more effective than traditional systems.

Document the positive results you observe through photos, anecdotal records, and data collection. Track the classroom climate, student engagement, academic progress, and office referrals to demonstrate your approach's effectiveness.

Create regular communication systems that keep families informed about their children's growth and classroom experiences. Send home positive notes, make celebratory phone calls, and share specific examples of students' contributions and progress. Nurture relationships with families so that when challenges arise, you can work together as partners.

Establish peer support networks with other educators who are interested in trauma-responsive practices. Share resources, problem-solve challenges together, and advocate collectively for systemic changes that support all students' social-emotional needs.

STEP 6: Reflect on and adjust your practices.

Dignity-preserving behavior support is not a program you implement but a way of being with students that requires ongoing reflection and refinement. Regularly assess your classroom climate and relationships through student feedback, family input, and your observations. Ask students what makes them feel safe and supported, what challenges they face, and what changes would help them be more successful.

Review your responses to challenging situations to identify patterns and areas for growth. Notice when you feel triggered or reactive, and develop strategies for staying regulated when students are struggling. Remember that your emotional state significantly impacts your ability to support students effectively.

Stay current with research and best practices in trauma-responsive education, social-emotional learning, and restorative practices. Continue learning through professional development, reading, and collaboration with colleagues who share your commitment to dignity-preserving approaches.

Advocate for systemic changes that support trauma-responsive practices throughout the school. Share your successes with administrators, participate in policy discussions, and work to create environments where all educators can implement healing-centered approaches without feeling isolated or unsupported.

OVERCOMING PUSHBACK

When you begin implementing trauma-responsive behavior practices, you will likely encounter questions and concerns from colleagues, administrators, and family members who are accustomed to traditional behavior management systems. Here's how to address the most common concerns while staying committed to protecting student dignity.

Parents want to know how their kid behaved today. How am I supposed to tell them without the daily folder? Establish relationships with families through regular positive communication rather than relying on behavior tracking systems. When concerns arise, address them through phone conversations or meetings where you can provide context and work together on solutions. Focus on building trust and partnership rather than on recording surveillance and "gotcha" moments. Most parents would rather hear, "Lydia showed incredible kindness today," than "Lydia stayed on green."

Our principal says we must use the school-wide behavior system for consistency across all classrooms. Work within your system while advocating for trauma-responsive approaches. Document the positive results you're seeing, share research on the effectiveness of trauma-responsive practices, and offer to pilot alternatives while tracking outcomes. Many administrators are open to change when they see data showing improved student engagement and reduced office referrals. Frame it as enhancing the existing system rather than replacing it entirely.

If I don't have consequences that other kids can see, how will they know I have expectations? Clear, consistent expectations don't require public shaming to be effective. Students learn appropriate behavior through explicit teaching, modeling, practice, and natural consequences. Public humiliation undermines respect for expectations by teaching that making mistakes results in social punishment rather than learning opportunities. Your expectations become stronger, not weaker, when students trust that you'll handle their struggles with dignity.

The other kids will notice that some students get different treatment, and they will complain that it's not fair. Teach students about fairness versus equity using analogies. "If someone has a broken leg, they get crutches. If someone is sick, they get medicine. We don't all get the same solutions because not everybody has the same needs. Everyone gets what they need to be successful." Normalize the idea that everyone's brain works differently and deserves appropriate support. Kids understand this concept better than most adults do.

You're letting kids get away with bad behavior and not holding them accountable. Distinguish between accountability and punishment. Holding students accountable means helping them understand the impact of their choices and taking action to make it right. Punishment focuses on making students suffer for their mistakes rather than learning from them. Restorative practices create deeper accountability than traditional consequences while preserving dignity and relationships. Plus, have you ever seen a behavior chart actually change a kid's behavior in the long term? We'll wait.

THE HACK IN ACTION

Let's follow Miss Kelley, a second-grade teacher who decided to eliminate the clip chart system that had dominated her classroom management for years. Initially, she worried about losing control and facing administrative pushback, but she was tired of watching her most vulnerable students suffer public humiliation daily.

Miss Kelley began by removing the clip chart and explaining to her students that she wanted to try a new approach to helping everyone be successful. She introduced the idea of making mistakes as learning opportunities and emphasized that everyone's brain worked differently and needed different kinds of support. Instead of tracking behavior publicly, Miss Kelley created a private system for noting both challenges and successes for each student. When problems arose, she addressed them through quiet conversations, often discovering underlying needs she'd previously missed when focused on chart management.

The transformation in her classroom climate was immediate. Students who had previously shut down or acted out when their clips moved began engaging more positively. Dimitri, who had spent most days on red, started participating in discussions and offering to help classmates. Pavarti, who had internalized that she was a "bad kid" based on her chart history, began seeing herself as someone who could contribute positively to the classroom community.

Most significantly, Miss Kelley found herself strengthening relationships with her students because she was no longer focused on catching them in mistakes. Instead, she was actively looking for their strengths and helping them develop skills for handling challenges. Lee, a recently adopted child with a refugee background, began to flourish under this approach. His adoptive family had been working hard to help him feel safe and valued, and Miss Kelley's healing-centered classroom became another space where he could build trust with caring adults. By spring, Lee was volunteering to help new students feel welcome and had become a peer mentor during group work.

When her principal asked about the missing behavior chart, Miss Kelley shared data showing decreased classroom disruptions, increased student engagement, and improved academic performance. She also asked her administrator to think about how many students she had sent to the office for behavior concerns (none). Miss Kelley explained her trauma-responsive approach and offered to document its effectiveness throughout the year.

By spring, Miss Kelley's classroom had become a model for other teachers interested in trauma-responsive practices. Her students demonstrated higher levels of intrinsic motivation, better peer relationships, and more sophisticated self-regulation skills than in previous years when external behavior systems dominated their daily experience.

When we ditch public behavior charts and embrace trauma-responsive, healing-centered practices, we do not lose accountability; we gain authenticity. We stop teaching students that their struggles are entertainment for others and start showing them that their growth matters more than their mistakes.

This shift requires us to believe that children are capable of developing intrinsic motivation and self-regulation when given appropriate support and respect. It means trusting that relationships and teaching are more powerful tools than shame and surveillance. The students who benefit the most from this approach are often those who have suffered the most under traditional behavior management systems—children whose trauma histories make them particularly vulnerable to shame and public humiliation. When we protect their dignity while maintaining high expectations, we create the safety they need to heal and grow.

Building classroom communities based on mutual respect rather than behavioral compliance improves the school climate and prepares students for lifelong success in relationships and work environments that value collaboration, intrinsic motivation, and authentic accountability. In the short term, we are changing how we manage student behavior; in the long term, we are changing how students see themselves and their capacity to contribute positively to the world.

REFLECTION
QUESTIONS

1. **What public systems in your classroom might be causing shame for vulnerable students?** Look beyond obvious behavior charts to consider other ways students' struggles might be broadcast or made visible to peers.

2. **How can you maintain high expectations while preserving student dignity?** Consider the difference between accountability and humiliation, and identify ways to address problems that build rather than break down relationships.

3. **What would need to change in your classroom culture to help students feel safe to make mistakes?** Think about how shifting from perfection-focused to growth-focused approaches might impact learning and community-building.

4. **Which students might be suffering the most under current behavior management systems?** Often, these are students with trauma histories who most need healing-centered approaches to develop trust and regulation skills.

HACK 4

EMPHASIZE RELATIONSHIPS BEFORE RIGOR

Connect Before You Correct

No significant learning can occur
without a significant relationship.
— DR. JAMES P. COMER, CHILD PSYCHIATRIST

THE DATA MEETING was going exactly as expected. Charts filled the conference room walls, showing reading levels, benchmark scores, and achievement gaps in stark black and white. Mx. Newman sat quietly as colleagues dissected their students' performance like specimens under a microscope.

"Third period is behind in comprehension," the literacy coach announced, pointing to a particularly discouraging graph. "We need to accelerate the students' progress immediately. More intervention blocks, additional practice packets, and extended reading time."

Mx. Newman raised their hand tentatively. "What if the problem isn't that the students can't read? What if it's that the kids don't feel safe enough to focus?"

The room went quiet. The assistant principal looked confused. "What do you mean?"

"I mean," Mx. Newman continued, "that half of these kids are dealing with trauma at home. Diego's parents are divorcing. Jenna just moved to her fourth foster placement this year. Eddie hasn't seen his dad in three months because of deployment. When I try to push more reading intervention, they shut down completely. But when we spend five minutes talking about their lives first, suddenly they can focus on the lesson."

The literacy coach shuffled her papers uncomfortably. "Well, yes, relationships matter, but we have curriculum to cover. These test scores won't improve themselves."

And there it was. The fundamental misunderstanding that's crushing both teachers and students. The belief that we must choose between caring and curriculum, between connection and content, between relationships and rigor. As if a child's emotional well-being and academic success exist in separate universes.

We've created an educational system that treats students like data points to be moved rather than human beings to be known. We measure everything except what matters most: the bond between teacher and student that makes all other learning possible.

For children affected by trauma, the relationships with their teachers aren't just nice to have; they are neurologically necessary. When a child's nervous system is stuck in survival mode, the child can't access higher-order thinking or engage in complex problem-solving because the brain is scanning for danger instead of looking for learning opportunities.

Yet, somehow, we've convinced ourselves that spending time on relationships takes time away from instruction. We act as if knowing our students as people is a luxury we can't afford when test scores are low. We treat emotional connection like an add-on rather than the foundation that makes everything else possible.

Here's what's really happening when we prioritize curriculum over connection: Students who don't feel safe or valued in our classrooms spend enormous amounts of mental energy managing their emotions, wondering if they belong, and protecting themselves from perceived threats. A student worried about whether his teacher likes him can't fully concentrate on long division. A child uncertain about her place in the classroom community can't take the intellectual risks that real learning requires.

WE CAN ENSURE STUDENTS FEEL KNOWN, VALUED, AND SAFE BEFORE WE ASK THEM TO TAKE INTELLECTUAL RISKS OR ENGAGE WITH CHALLENGING CONTENT.

Children who have been in the foster care system face particularly complex challenges in forming connections with teachers. They've learned that adults come and go, that "permanent" might not mean permanent, and that opening their hearts to caring adults often leads to pain when those relationships end. These students need teachers who understand their hesitation to trust while consistently demonstrating safety and reliability.

The irony is crushing. In our rush to cover content, we're making learning *less* likely to happen. When students don't feel connected to their teachers, engagement drops, behavior problems increase, and academic progress stalls. We're sacrificing relationships for academic achievement, making it even harder to attain.

Think about your learning experiences. Who were the teachers who impacted your life? Chances are, they weren't necessarily the ones who covered the most curriculum or assigned the most homework. They were the ones who saw you, believed in you, and made you feel like you mattered. They were the teachers who connected with you as a person before trying to fill you with content (and probably the ones who didn't make you feel like a walking test score).

We've created a false urgency around curriculum coverage that makes teachers feel guilty about spending time on relationship-building. They worry that colleagues will judge them for wasting time on social-emotional connections. They fear administrators will question their focus if students are laughing, sharing, or being "human" during instructional time. Heaven forbid that children are enjoying learning.

But what if we've got it completely backward? What if the time we spend on relationships isn't time taken away from learning but time invested in making learning possible? What if connection isn't the enemy of achievement but is its greatest ally?

THE HACK: EMPHASIZE RELATIONSHIPS BEFORE RIGOR

Educators don't have to choose between relationships and academics; they're not separate entities competing for our time and attention. Relationships are the foundation that makes rigorous learning possible. When we invest in connection first, teaching and learning become easier and more effective.

This Hack requires a fundamental shift in how we think about teaching. Instead of seeing relationship-building as an activity we do in addition to instruction, we see it as the precondition that makes instruction meaningful. Instead of viewing connection as time away from learning, we understand it as the pathway to deeper, more sustainable learning.

The Core Strategy: Start with Meaningful Connections

The core strategy is simple in concept but revolutionary in practice. We must connect before we correct. We must build bridges before boosting benchmarks. We can ensure students feel known, valued, and safe before we ask them to take intellectual risks or engage with challenging content.

When we prioritize relationships, we're teaching in a scientifically sound way. Trauma-affected brains often can't access higher-order thinking because they feel unsafe, so a connection with a trusted adult becomes the bridge that moves students from survival mode back to learning mode. This is especially crucial, as students who have been exposed to trauma often have nervous systems that have been conditioned to expect danger from adult relationships.

Learning to read student cues for needing connection develops with practice and intentional observation. Watch for physical indicators, such as slumped shoulders, avoiding eye contact, or sudden changes in energy levels. Behavioral shifts often reflect relationship needs, too. The compliant student who becomes argumentative might be testing whether you'll still care when she's not perfect. The class clown who withdraws could be signaling that his usual strategies aren't working.

Pay attention to patterns of student disconnects. Some struggle on Fridays due to elevated worries about the weekend; others struggle during subjects that trigger anxiety. Listen carefully to what students share, both directly and indirectly. The student who shares that a parent is stressed might need extra support that day. Notice changes in peer interactions as another indicator, especially students who suddenly seem isolated or involved in more conflicts.

Connection as Academic Strategy

A powerful way to develop relationships while maintaining academic focus is to harness students' natural desire to communicate and connect with one another. Instead of seeing student conversation as a behavior to manage, we can transform it into an intentional learning tool that serves multiple purposes simultaneously.

Traditional classrooms often operate under the assumption that talking equals disruption, and silence equals learning. But the opposite can be true. Students need opportunities to process information verbally, share ideas with peers, and gain understanding through dialogue. When we create a structure and space for academic conversation, we're improving learning outcomes and cultivating community and peer relationships. It turns out the thing we've been trying to stop is the thing that helps students learn.

For children affected by trauma, structured conversations provide safe ways to connect with peers and share their thinking without being put on the spot. A student with social anxiety might thrive in paired discussions. A child who has been in the foster care system and is hesitant to speak up in large group settings might contribute to collaborative problem-solving activities.

Every subject area offers opportunities to learn about students as individuals while maintaining instructional focus. Reading conferences become chances to understand students' interests, experiences, and perspectives. Writing workshops reveal students' voices, concerns, and dreams. Number talks offer windows into children's reasoning strategies. Science investigations show how students think and approach problems. Social studies discussions uncover students' values and worldviews.

The key is to approach content with genuine curiosity about how each student experiences and connects with the material. Instead of focusing solely on whether students understand the lesson, we can also pay attention to what the lesson reveals about who they are as learners and people.

Relationships thrive on authentic interest rather than superficial pleasantries, meaning we can learn about students' stories as well as their names. Students can tell the difference between a teacher who genuinely cares about their lives and one who's going through the motions. The magic happens when we move beyond surface-level interactions to know each child as a unique individual.

Relationship-building can't be confined to designated times or specific activities. We need to weave it throughout the school day, both in planned and spontaneous ways. Morning greetings become opportunities to check in and set a positive tone. Transitions offer moments for individual connections. Lunch conversations reveal interests and personalities. After-school time allows for deeper relationship-building.

The goal is to create multiple chances each day for every student to feel seen, heard, and valued. Some students connect through academic discussions, others through shared interests, and still others through simply feeling understood during difficult moments.

Cultivate Relationships with Difficult-to-Reach Students

Some students resist every connection attempt, yet they often need relationships the most. Their past experiences have taught them that opening up to adults leads to disappointment or hurt.

Start by examining your assumptions. "Antisocial" students might be protecting themselves from rejection. "Disrespectful" children could be testing whether you'll abandon them like others have. "Lazy" kiddos might be too afraid to fail, so why bother at all? Meet these students where they are rather than where you think they should be.

Find small, nonthreatening ways to show you care. Leave a positive note on their desks, share comments related to their interests, and offer choices, such as letting them decide where to sit as they complete their assignments or whether they want to work with a partner or solo. These micro-connections gradually increase trust without triggering defensive reactions.

Look for each student's hidden strengths and interests. The disruptive student might be a natural leader who needs appropriate outlets. The withdrawn child might be highly observant and thoughtful. Be patient with the process and celebrate small victories, such as when the student makes eye contact for the first time or shares a personal detail.

Remember that these students often test your commitment to the relationship. They might get worse before they get better as they challenge you to prove you won't give up on them. They don't want to push you away; instead, they want to make sure you won't walk away. Stay consistent, maintain kind boundaries, and continue to show up emotionally, even when it's difficult.

WHAT **YOU** CAN DO TOMORROW

Ready to start putting relationships at the center of your classroom practice? These immediate actions will begin transforming your classroom culture while maintaining academic focus. Building connections doesn't require overhauling your entire approach; it requires purposeful attention to the human beings in your care.

- **Create a connection-tracking system for yourself.** Develop a basic checklist or note-taking system using your laptop, tablet, or phone to track meaningful interactions with each student. Doing so helps ensure quieter students don't get overlooked while more demanding students get all your attention. Start by identifying which students you connected with today and create a plan for who you will focus on tomorrow.

- **Use transition times for micro-connections.** Those brief moments between activities are perfect for quick relationship-building. Try specific observations like, "I love that graphic novel you're carrying, Toby!" while students line up, or "Did you finish that collage you were working on, Sue?" while passing out papers. These fifteen-second conversations add up to meaningful relationships over time.

- **Have a genuine conversation with your most challenging students.** Often, the students who push our buttons the hardest are the ones who need connection the most. Find a moment to engage them in authentic dialogue about topics they care about. You might discover that underneath the challenging behavior are children longing to be understood. Ask about their passions, their experiences, or what matters to them. Be ready to research unfamiliar topics. Letting the child know that you read more about a subject they care about further cements that you are engaged and invested in the relationship.

- **Notice and comment on one positive action by each student tomorrow.** Develop the habit of actively looking for strengths, contributions, or growth moments. Stating "I noticed how thoughtfully you listened during our discussion" or "You showed real persistence with that math problem" helps students see themselves through your appreciative eyes.

- **Schedule a brief individual check-in with one student who seems disconnected.** Choose a student who appears withdrawn, stressed, or disengaged and find two minutes to connect privately. Ask how they're doing, what's on their mind, or what would help them feel more successful in your classroom. All children want to feel valued and heard. These check-ins can be the start of helping them feel comfortable talking with you if they are in need.

A BLUEPRINT FOR FULL IMPLEMENTATION

Offering a classroom culture where relationships and rigor work together requires systematic planning and consistent implementation. You're recognizing that connection and content strengthen each other when woven together thoughtfully. Here are the steps to create an environment where every student feels known, valued, and academically challenged.

STEP 1: Create morning greeting rituals that connect with each child personally.

Develop systems that ensure every student feels welcomed and noticed each day. Establish a morning routine where you stand at your classroom door to greet students individually. This gives you a brief but meaningful one-on-one interaction time with each child.

The key is making these check-ins authentic rather than perfunctory. Instead of a generic "Good morning!" try remembering details from previous conversations, such as "How's your baby brother feeling today, Marie? You mentioned he was sick yesterday." Show genuine interest in their responses and follow up on topics that matter to them. It's the difference between connecting as a human and turning into a greeting robot programmed with basic pleasantries.

Consider different greeting styles for different students. Some children love high-fives and enthusiastic hellos, while others prefer quiet acknowledgments or gentle questions. Pay attention to what makes each child light up, and adjust accordingly. For younger children, you might include a visual with options for saying, "Good morning!" Older children can create a personalized list of greetings they are most comfortable with, like a peace sign, fist bump, or nod. For students who arrive late or seem stressed, have a calm backup greeting ready that doesn't draw unwanted attention.

THE STUDENTS WHO PUSH OUR BUTTONS THE HARDEST ARE THE ONES WHO NEED CONNECTION THE MOST.

These arrival rituals are essential for children affected by trauma, who may arrive at school already dysregulated from difficult home situations. Consistent, caring greetings signal safety and help students transition from survival mode to learning mode.

STEP 2: Build intentional conversations into academic content across all subject areas.

Systematically examine your curriculum to identify natural places for structured academic discussions. Literature circles become chances for students to share personal connections to characters and themes. Science investigations offer opportunities for collaborative observation and hypothesis-building. Social studies inquiries encourage perspective-sharing and discussions that foster critical thinking. Math lessons include time for students to justify their answers and learn from different problem-solving approaches.

Use what you know about students' interests to inform your teaching choices. If several students love animals, choose science texts about wildlife. If three students are passionate about comic books, let them compare superhero abilities using ratios. Or create assignments that allow for individualization, such as research projects with specific criteria and guidelines but flexible, student-selected topics. When students see their interests reflected in academic content, engagement soars and relationships deepen.

Create conversation protocols that ensure equity and engagement. Use strategies like think-pair-share, where everyone gets a chance to process alone and then with a partner before large group discussions. Try fishbowl conversations where some students demonstrate strong academic dialogue while others observe and learn. Jigsaw activities, where students become "experts" in skills and then share with a small group, ensure everyone contributes to discussions.

Design conversation prompts that connect academic content to student experiences. Instead of asking, "What did you think of this character?" try "Which character reminds you of someone in your life, and why?" Rather than "What caused this historical event?" ask, "How do you think people your age would have felt during this time period?"

Academic conversations that honor student experiences are especially powerful for those affected by trauma, who may feel their voices don't matter. When students see their perspectives valued in academic settings, it helps rebuild their sense of worth and belonging.

STEP 3: Use collaborative learning structures that foster peer relationships while advancing academic goals.

Design lessons that naturally encourage positive interactions between students. Partner work, small-group investigations, peer editing sessions, collaborative projects, and role-based discussions create opportunities for students to know each other as learners and individuals while engaging with rigorous content.

For children affected by trauma, positive peer relationships can be as healing as teacher-student connections. Children who have been in the foster care system, in particular, benefit from seeing that other kids accept and enjoy them, helping them believe they're worthy of friendship and belonging.

However, successful collaboration doesn't happen automatically. Educators may have to teach collaboration skills explicitly. Trauma can impact how children pick up on nonverbal cues and navigate social communication, so provide direct instruction in sharing ideas respectfully, listening actively, dividing tasks fairly, and supporting teammates. These strategies can also benefit children with social communication challenges, such as those with an autism spectrum disorder, ADHD, or a nonverbal learning disability. Practice these skills through low-stakes activities before applying them to major projects.

Create group formation strategies that support relationship-building. Mix up partnerships regularly so students get to know different classmates, but also let them choose their go-to people to ensure they are comfortable and at ease. When you are forming groups, consider compatibility for students who struggle socially, and provide extra support during collaborative activities for those who find peer interaction challenging. When pairing up students, make sure that one person does not do all the work while the other listens. The goal is a dialogue, not a monologue.

These collaborative experiences are especially healing for students affected by trauma, who may have learned that relationships are unsafe or unreliable. Positive peer interactions in structured settings help rebuild their capacity for healthy connections.

STEP 4: Train students in productive academic conversation and social interaction skills.

Give students the tools they need for productive academic conversation skills. Teach them sentence starters like, "I agree with what you said about … and I'd like to add …," or "That's interesting, but I see it differently because …," as well as open-ended questions, such as, "How did you come up with that solution?" or "Why do you think that happened?" These supports help students engage in respectful dialogue while processing content more deeply.

Explicitly teach students how to have respectful, engaging discussions about academic content. Consider the skills that are necessary for these types of discussions: listening actively, asking thoughtful questions, and disagreeing respectfully. To teach each one, model the words and behaviors students should use through demonstrations and think-alouds. Then, give students ample time to role-play examples of classroom discussions. Finally, provide individualized support for students as they try their newly learned skills. Teaching students how to have respectful and engaging discussions, especially when disagreeing, improves learning outcomes, communication skills, and relationships throughout the day. (To learn more about how to break down conflict and build consensus in a polarized world, see the book *Preventing Polarization* by Michelle Blanchet and Brian Deters.)

Practice conversation skills through structured activities, such as hot seat, where a student takes on the role of a book character or historical figure. The student sits in the "hot seat" at the front of the room while the rest of the class asks questions. The student must respond as the character or historical figure, using evidence from the text or background knowledge.

Create anchor charts or individual reference cards that support student conversations. Post sentence starters for academic discussions, guidelines for respectful disagreement, and steps for collaborative problem-solving. Include visuals to support non-readers, children with reading challenges, and English learners. Make these tools accessible during all collaborative activities.

Provide differentiated conversation support for learners. Some students need extra processing time before speaking, others benefit from movement while talking, and still others require visual supports to organize their thinking. Offer multiple ways for students to participate in academic conversations so everyone can contribute meaningfully. Help students recognize that we all have different communication styles and strengths, and that's what makes our classroom community interesting and diverse.

These communication skills are particularly empowering for children affected by trauma, who may have learned that their voices don't matter. Teaching students how to express themselves respectfully gives them agency and helps them advocate for their needs.

STEP 5: Design systems for ongoing relationship maintenance and growth throughout the year.

Relationships require ongoing attention and nurturing beyond initial connection-tracking. Make deeper connections possible in your classroom through weekly community circles where students can share celebrations and challenges, monthly individual conferences focused on both academic and personal growth, quarterly goal-setting conversations that include social-emotional objectives, and seasonal class meetings to address community issues and celebrate successes.

Establish sustainable relationship-building practices that don't overwhelm your schedule. Some teachers arrange for rotating lunch conversations with different students, others create "special helper" rotations that give one-on-one time, and still others use transition times for individual check-ins. The key is to create predictable times to deepen relationships.

Document relationship growth and challenges to inform your practice. Note which students seem more engaged after relationship-building efforts, track behavioral changes that correlate with connection activities, and record successful strategies for developing trust with specific students.

OVERCOMING PUSHBACK

When you start prioritizing relationships alongside academics, some colleagues, administrators, or parents may question whether you're being rigorous enough. These concerns usually stem from the false belief that care and high expectations can't coexist. Here's how to address common worries while staying committed to relationship-first teaching.

I don't have time for relationships with all these curriculum demands. This concern assumes relationships steal precious minutes from learning, but the opposite is true. Students learn more efficiently when they feel connected to their teachers. Time invested in relationships turbocharges academic progress by increasing engagement, motivation, and the willingness to take intellectual risks. It's like complaining that you don't have time to put gas in your car because you're too busy driving.

Document the academic benefits you see when relationships improve. Track engagement levels, behavior incidents, and learning outcomes. Share stories about students who made breakthrough progress once they felt valued and connected. Help others see that relationships aren't sabotaging academics but supercharging them.

I'm not a counselor, and I didn't sign up to be a therapist. True, but fostering caring teacher-student relationships is entirely different from providing therapy. You're not trying to fix students' psychological issues or provide clinical interventions. You're simply creating the emotionally safe environment that all children need in order to learn effectively, which is part of high-quality teaching.

The difference is significant. Counselors and therapists work on healing trauma and addressing mental health needs. Teachers build relationships that make learning possible. Both roles matter, and they're distinct. Caring about students' well-being and creating classroom communities where children feel valued isn't therapy; it's teaching done right.

Student talk creates chaos and prevents real learning. This objection comes from a misunderstanding about how humans learn. Most people, especially students in PreK–12, need to process information verbally, share ideas, and gain understanding through dialogue. When conversation is structured and purposeful, it enhances learning rather than creates the academic apocalypse some fear.

Share information about the learning benefits of academic discussion. Show colleagues how structured conversation improves comprehension, critical thinking, and retention. Demonstrate that purposeful talk supports academic goals rather than turning your classroom into a three-ring circus. Invite your administrator to visit your classroom when students are engaged in productive academic conversations.

They have to learn classroom expectations and self-control. While students do need to know the appropriate times for silence and the importance of listening, they also need to develop communication skills, collaboration abilities, and critical-thinking capacities. A classroom that only values compliance is not preparing students for their futures.

Modern workplaces require people who can express ideas effectively, solve problems creatively, and engage with others constructively. These skills develop through practice, not through suppression. When we teach students to engage in respectful academic discourse, we're preparing them for future success, not undermining their ability to follow directions.

THE HACK IN ACTION

Mrs. Thomas inherited a fourth-grade class with a reputation for being difficult. Previous teachers had focused on strict behavior management and intensive academic interventions; however, engagement remained low, and disruptions were frequent. Students seemed disconnected from each other and suspicious of adult authority.

Mrs. Thomas decided to start the year differently. Instead of jumping into academic routines, she spent the first two weeks learning about each student as an individual. She discovered that Jane loved astronomy, Aimee was passionate about horses, and John had an encyclopedic knowledge of sports statistics.

She began incorporating student interests into academic lessons. Math word problems featured baseball statistics for John and horse racing for Aimee. Science units connected to Jane's fascination with space. Reading selections included topics that matched the various passions of different students.

More importantly, she transformed her instruction to include regular academic conversations. Instead of silent reading followed by individual comprehension questions, students engaged in book talks with discussion partners. Math lessons included time for students to explain their thinking to peers. Science investigations became collaborative explorations.

The transformation was remarkable. Students who had been labeled as "behavior problems" became engaged learners when their interests were honored and their voices were valued.

Academic discussions revealed a depth of thinking that had been hidden behind compliance-focused teaching. The classroom community strengthened as students learned to appreciate each other's perspectives and expertise.

By the end of the year, Mrs. Thomas's students had made significant academic gains and developed confidence, curiosity, and caring relationships with each other and their teacher. She had proved that prioritizing relationships didn't lower academic expectations; it created the foundation that made higher achievement possible.

In middle school, Mr. Teagarden faced a different challenge. His seventh-grade language arts students were academically capable but socially fragmented and emotionally guarded. Many seemed to view school as a requirement to endure rather than embrace, and peer relationships were often negative or superficial.

Mr. Teagarden recognized that middle schoolers desperately need to feel understood and accepted, but they're also naturally suspicious of adult attempts to connect. He decided to develop relationships through the content itself, using literature as a bridge to understand his students' experiences and perspectives.

When reading novels with complex characters, he encouraged students to connect personally with the stories. Instead of traditional book reports, students engaged in character analysis discussions that naturally led to sharing their own experiences and insights. Writing workshops became chances for students to explore their voices and stories.

He established book clubs where students could choose texts that interested them and engage in small-group discussions with peers who shared similar reading preferences. These conversations revealed students' values, experiences, and dreams while building genuine connections between classmates.

Mr. Teagarden also created weekly community circles where students could share what was happening in their lives, celebrate successes, and process challenges. For students carrying heavy emotional backpacks, these circles became meaningful parts of the week, giving them a safe forum to be authentic with each other.

The results extended far beyond the classroom. Students who had been isolated found friend groups. Academic engagement increased as students felt more invested in the classroom community. Writing became more authentic and powerful as students felt safe sharing their genuine thoughts and experiences.

When we put relationships before rigor, we discover that they're not competing priorities but complementary forces. Students who feel known, valued, and safe become willing to take the intellectual risks that real learning requires. They engage more deeply with content because they trust the adult guiding their learning. They persist through challenges because they believe someone is invested in their success.

This process involves creating the conditions where high expectations become achievable. When students feel emotionally safe and personally connected to their teachers, they can access the parts of their brains responsible for complex thinking, creative problem-solving, and deep learning.

The beautiful irony is that prioritizing relationships accelerates academic progress rather than slows it down. Students who trust their teachers learn more efficiently. Children who feel valued in classroom communities take bigger intellectual risks. Kids who know their voices matter engage more authentically with content.

For students exposed to trauma, the teacher relationship often becomes the foundation of all other healing and growth. When these children experience unconditional acceptance and genuine care from a trusted adult, they begin to believe that they're worthy of love and capable of success. That belief becomes the bedrock on which everything else is built.

REFLECTION
QUESTIONS

1. **How well do you know each student as a whole person beyond academic performance?** Consider what you know about each student's interests, family situations, dreams, and challenges outside of school.

2. **How are you using student conversation and collaboration to support learning and relationship-building?** Look for opportunities to transform individual work into a meaningful dialogue that serves multiple purposes.

3. **What gets in the way of your connecting with certain students?** Honestly examine whether personal triggers, unconscious biases, or systemic pressures interfere with relationship-building.

4. **Where can you add more intentional academic conversations that honor student voices while advancing learning objectives?** Identify specific lessons or activities that could benefit from collaborative discussion and structured dialogue.

5. **How do your relationships with students impact their willingness to take intellectual risks and engage with challenging content?** Consider the connection between emotional safety and academic courage in your classroom.

CREATE CALMING PHYSICAL ENVIRONMENTS

Design Low-Sensory, Regulation-Supporting Areas

Your classroom environment speaks to your students before you utter a single word. What is your classroom saying?
— MEGAN DREDGE, EDUCATOR AND AUTHOR

EIGHT-YEAR-OLD FATIMA WALKED into her new classroom on the first day of school and immediately felt her chest tighten. Everywhere she looked, a display or decoration was demanding her attention. Alphabet strips marched around the room at eye level. Math anchor charts competed with reading posters for wall space. A behavior chart blazed in neon colors near the door. Word walls sprouted from every available surface like academic kudzu. The fluorescent lights hummed overhead, casting everything in a harsh, hospital-like glow.

Within ten minutes, Fatima was under her desk.

Her teacher, Mrs. Martin, crouched down beside her. "What's wrong, sweetie?"

"It's too much," Fatima whispered, hands pressed against her ears. "Everything is too loud and too bright and too busy. My brain can't turn off."

What Mrs. Martin didn't know was that Fatima had recently been reunited with her mother after escaping a domestic violence situation. Her trauma history had left her hypervigilant, constantly scanning for threats. In a classroom designed to be stimulating and engaging, Fatima's brain interpreted every colorful poster and busy bulletin board as requiring immediate attention and analysis. Her developing nervous system, already primed for danger, couldn't relax enough to focus on learning.

Mrs. Martin looked around her classroom with new eyes. What she had thought was an exciting, resource-rich learning environment suddenly looked like sensory assault. Every well-meaning placement of an educational poster and cheerful decoration was competing for the attention of children whose brains were already working overtime just to feel safe.

That afternoon, Mrs. Martin started taking things down.

THE PROBLEM: WE'RE OVERSTIMULATING OUR STUDENTS

Walk into most elementary classrooms, and you'll find yourself in what we like to call "Pinterest paradise." Every inch of wall space is covered with educational posters, student work, anchor charts, word walls, number lines, behavior charts, and motivational quotes. The ceiling might sport hanging decorations, and the bulletin boards change monthly to match the current theme. Teachers spend hours creating these displays, believing they're creating rich learning environments.

But here's what we've learned about sensory processing. For many of our students, especially those who've experienced trauma, these well-intentioned classroom decorations create the opposite effect than the one we're hoping for. Instead of supporting learning, they're making it harder for vulnerable children to regulate their nervous systems and focus on instruction.

Children who've experienced trauma often have heightened sensory sensitivities. Their internal alarm systems are already working overtime, detecting signs of danger and trying to process multiple streams of information simultaneously. When we surround them with visual stimulation, we're essentially asking their already overwhelmed brains to process even more information before they can focus on learning.

And what about noise? Hard surfaces reflect sound, creating echoes and amplifying every pencil drop, chair scrape, and whispered conversation. For children whose trauma has made them sensitive to sudden sounds or who use auditory processing to monitor their safety, these acoustic environments can be exhausting.

Think about the last time you tried to have a critical phone conversation in a noisy restaurant. You probably found yourself getting distracted by conversations at other tables, the clinking of dishes, and the general chaos around you. Now imagine that a similar level of distraction is how many of our students affected by trauma experience our classrooms every day. The difference is that they can't leave the restaurant.

The irony is crushing. In our effort to create engaging and stimulating environments, we've created spaces that prevent our most vulnerable students from focusing on the learning. We've turned our classrooms into sensory obstacle courses that students must navigate before they can begin to focus on instruction.

THE HACK: CREATE CALMING PHYSICAL ENVIRONMENTS

The solution isn't to create sterile, boring classrooms that look like prison cells. It's to design learning spaces that support nervous system regulation while still providing the resources students need to succeed. When we create environments that help children feel calm and focused, we're not removing rigor; we're removing barriers.

This Hack requires us to think about classroom design through the lens of neuroscience and trauma-responsive practices. Instead of asking, "How can I display as much educational content as possible?" we can ask, "How can I create a space that supports all my students' readiness to learn?"

The Core Strategy: Design for Regulation

When it comes to the physical design of our classrooms, our focus should be on prioritizing regulation over stimulation. We can make thoughtful choices about lighting, reduce visual clutter, incorporate calming elements, and create spaces where students can regulate their emotions when needed.

Use Soft, Natural Lighting When Possible

Lighting dramatically impacts mood, alertness, focus, and overall well-being. Consider the harsh fluorescent lights that are humming and flickering throughout our schools, and many are operating at frequencies that can trigger headaches, anxiety, and concentration difficulties for students with sensitivities. Some children with trauma histories or sensory processing difficulties find fluorescent lighting particularly painful or emotionally dysregulating.

Natural light, when available, provides the ideal learning environment because it reduces eye strain and feels more comfortable to the eyes than artificial light. It also triggers the release of serotonin, the feel-good hormone, while reducing cortisol, the stress hormone. Natural light often feels relaxing and restorative. It brightens the room and helps children and adults find their sense of calm.

Table lamps, floor lamps, or twinkle lights (decorative, flickering lights often used during the holidays) with warm or soft white bulbs can transform the feeling of a classroom from over-stimulating to welcoming. String lights hung from the ceiling or around bulletin boards create a magical, calming ambiance that many younger students find comforting and even enchanting. Many teachers discover that students are noticeably calmer and more focused when harsh overhead lighting is replaced with softer alternatives. You might be amazed at how different your classroom feels when you turn off those fluorescent lights and flip on a few well-placed lamps or string lights instead.

Strategically Minimize Visual Clutter

We can be intentional about what visual information serves our current learning goals without having to leave walls blank. Instead of permanent displays that become background noise, create focused display areas for information that students are actively using.

Consider the twenty-foot rule when creating displays. If students can't read or use the information from twenty feet away, it's probably not serving its intended purpose and is just adding to visual clutter. Make sure students can read the text from their seats, and limit the amount of information competing for their attention in one spot.

Use solid, neutral backgrounds for displays rather than bright, patterned papers that compete with the content. When every bulletin board screams for attention with neon borders and busy backgrounds, nothing gets the focus it deserves. Think of your wall displays like a well-designed website where less visual noise helps essential information stand out. Include white space, or empty areas around and between displays, to give your students' (and your own) eyes a rest.

> EVERY CLASSROOM NEEDS AT LEAST ONE AREA WHERE STUDENTS CAN GO TO CALM DOWN AND RESET WITHOUT SHAME OR PUNISHMENT.

Empty picture frames mounted on walls create perfect, organized spaces for displaying student work. When children's assignments, projects, or artwork are framed, it looks intentional and valued rather than randomly taped up. Don't worry about finding matching frames at garage sales. Mismatched frames can add character and charm while still creating an organized gallery feel. Or, if you really want a matching set, spray-paint them a neutral color like black, white, or brown.

Rotate displays based on current learning rather than trying to show everything all the time. If students are working on graphing this week, the data collection anchor chart should be prominently displayed, while the last unit's measurement poster can be stored away. This keeps walls current and purposeful while reducing visual competition.

Create Quiet Regulation Spaces

Every classroom needs at least one area where students can go to calm down and reset without shame or punishment—not a time-out corner or consequence area, but a wellness space that communicates that taking care of your emotional needs is smart.

These self-regulation spaces don't need to be large or expensive. A corner with soft seating, perhaps a beanbag or cushions, along with soothing materials like books, fidgets, stuffed animals, or stress balls, can provide exactly what overwhelmed students need. Older students might prefer access to journals, affirmation cards, and quiet activities like coloring books. Some teachers include noise-canceling headphones, cards with breathing exercises, or soft textures that provide sensory comfort. Pay attention to what individual students find calming, and adjust accordingly.

Incorporate Natural Elements

Bringing nature indoors has powerful calming effects on students. Plants improve air quality and enhance mental well-being. An aquarium can bring a touch of nature into your classroom while offering a relaxing, sensory-rich experience. The fish swimming slowly, the gentle bubbling sounds, and the soft glowing light can be soothing for many children. Easy-to-care-for terrarium pets, including snails, hermit crabs, and earthworms, incorporate nature and provide a quiet companionship, which is especially comforting for children who have experienced trauma.

Natural elements don't have to be expensive or store-bought. Tree branches suspended from the ceiling can display student work with clips while also serving as natural room dividers when light fabric is draped over them. Tree stumps make excellent alternative seating that students love. You might find these free on the side of the road after storms or by asking neighbors who've had tree work done. Smooth stones, interesting pieces of driftwood, or shells collected from nature walks can provide tactile comfort. Some teachers create nature tables with rotating seasonal items that students can explore during their free time.

Natural sounds can also contribute to a calming environment. Soft background sounds of rain, ocean waves, or forest ambiance played at low volumes can mask distracting noises while providing auditory comfort. (We'll talk more about music tempo in Hack 7.)

Consider Acoustics and Noise Management

Sound travels differently in every classroom, and managing acoustic environments is crucial for student focus and regulation. Hard surfaces amplify noise, while soft materials absorb sound and create more peaceful learning environments. Strategically placed sound-absorbing materials, including rugs, curtains, fabric wall hangings, or bookshelves, can significantly reduce noise levels and create more comfortable acoustic environments.

Be mindful of noise levels throughout the day, and adjust activities accordingly. If students seem overstimulated after recess or lunch, plan quieter activities to help them regulate rather than jumping into high-energy lessons. Pay attention to times when your classroom naturally becomes louder, and consider environmental modifications that might help.

WHAT YOU CAN DO TOMORROW

Ready to transform your classroom into a more calming, regulation-supporting environment? You can implement these changes right away, and they will have an instant impact on the feeling of your space. Start with one or two modifications, and observe how your students respond before making additional changes.

- **Do a three-minute declutter sweep.** Stand in your doorway and scan your classroom like you've never seen it before. Grab a bin or basket and remove five items from walls or flat surfaces that aren't currently helping kids learn. Old anchor charts? Expired reminders? Visual noise? Bye! You don't have to throw them away; just get them out of everyone's line of sight. Focus on areas where students' eyes naturally land first when they enter the room.

- **Invite students into the process.** Ask your students: "What's one thing in our classroom that helps your brain feel calm?" and "What's one thing that feels like *too much*?" You can have them answer aloud, on sticky notes, or as a response to a journal prompt. Their answers will guide your next steps and help them feel invested in creating a peaceful and welcoming classroom. You might be surprised by what they notice that you've overlooked or how differently they experience the space.

- **Make a regulation grab basket.** Collect items you already have scattered around your room—stress balls, fidgets, a few calming books, or small comfort items. Add simple glitter bottles (a plastic bottle, water, glitter, and a drop of glue) and write basic breathing exercises on index cards. For older students, you might add mandala or zentangle color sheets with colored pencils or felt-tip pens to color for stress relief. Put everything in one basket labeled Brain Break Tools or Feeling Helpers. Place it where students can access it independently when they need emotional support.

- **Introduce a low-maintenance plant.** Select a plant based on the available light and space, and your plant-care experience. Snake plants, spider plants, ZZ plants, and pothos are easy to grow and ideal for beginners. These choices are also hardy, thriving in a variety of light and temperature conditions. They can tolerate infrequent watering and neglect, making them perfect for busy teachers who don't have extra time to spend caring for flora. Of course, students can help with watering, pruning, and dusting to practice having responsibility.

- **Rearrange seating to match your teaching goals.** If you want students to collaborate, arrange desks in clusters. If you need them to focus independently, create more individual spaces. Your furniture arrangement should support the type of learning that takes place in the room. Notice how different arrangements affect student behavior and interaction patterns.

- **Add a teacher regulation cue.** Tape a sticky note to your desk that says, "Calm is contagious." Let that guide your energy, tone, and classroom transitions throughout the day. Your regulated presence becomes a calming influence on the entire classroom community. When you feel yourself getting rushed or stressed, glance at that reminder and take a breath before responding to students.

A BLUEPRINT FOR FULL IMPLEMENTATION

Creating a comprehensively calming classroom environment requires systematic attention to multiple sensory inputs and environmental factors. Rather than choosing and making one dramatic change, thoughtfully address lighting, visual design, acoustics, and spatial organization to support every student's nervous system needs. Here's your roadmap to transforming your space into one that helps students feel settled and ready to learn.

STEP 1: Assess your environment for sensory overload.

Begin by conducting an honest audit of your classroom from a student's perspective. Choose one student's desk to sit at and assess the view. Look up. What's competing for your attention? What's helping you stay focused? What feels like too much? Count how many separate displays, posters, charts, and decorations compete for focus in any single line of sight. Consider the lighting quality, noise levels, and overall feeling of the space.

This experiment gives you that child's perspective on visual noise and helps you understand what one student experiences every day. Try different seats throughout the week to get various viewpoints, especially from students who seem the most distracted or dysregulated.

Take photos of your classroom from different angles and examine them critically. Sometimes, we become blind to the visual chaos we've created because we see it every day. Fresh eyes on photos often reveal overwhelming elements we've stopped noticing.

Ask yourself these key questions as you assess: Can students' eyes find places to rest and focus? Does anything flash, blink, or move in distracting ways? Are there too many colors competing for attention? Is the text large enough for students to read from their seating areas? How does the space feel emotionally?

Consider inviting a trusted colleague to assess your classroom and provide feedback about the sensory environment. Sometimes, an outside perspective can identify overwhelming elements that we've become accustomed to seeing.

STEP 2: Make strategic lighting adjustments.

Develop a comprehensive lighting plan that supports learning and regulation throughout the day. Try turning off the fluorescent overhead lights to see what additional lights are necessary. If you have windows, arrange your classroom to maximize natural light while minimizing glare or harsh contrasts. Hang curtains or blinds to adjust lighting levels as needed throughout the day. Clean windows regularly and avoid blocking them with displays or furniture.

DEVELOP CLEAR CRITERIA FOR WHAT DESERVES SPACE IN YOUR CLASSROOM, AND DISPLAY ONLY WHAT STUDENTS ACTIVELY NEED FOR THEIR CURRENT LEARNING GOALS.

In rooms that need additional lighting, or during darker months and on overcast days, experiment with alternatives to fluorescent overheads. You don't need to spend a fortune on classroom lighting. Check garage sales, antique shops, or thrift stores for affordable lamps. Post on social media, asking if friends or neighbors have extra lamps they're not using. Many people have a few stored away that they'd happily share with a teacher. Twinkle lights are an inexpensive option that creates a magical ambiance when strung around the room or on bulletin boards.

Consider the changing lighting needs throughout the day. Morning activities might benefit from brighter lighting to help students wake up and focus, while afternoon lessons might work better with softer lighting that prevents overstimulation. Some teachers use different lighting for different types of activities—brighter lights for detailed work and dimmer lights for discussions or storytelling.

Create lighting zones within your classroom, if possible. Having different lighting levels in various areas allows students to choose environments that support their current needs and tasks. A brighter area might be perfect for reading, while a softer zone works better for reflection or calming activities. Some children, including those who have experienced trauma, might crave the sensory input of bright lights to feel grounded or in control. Having an area of the room void of dim lights and shadows might feel safer for them.

STEP 3: Organize and minimize visual clutter systematically.

Develop clear criteria for what deserves space in your classroom, and display only what students actively need for their current learning goals. Everything else should be stored away until needed, reducing visual competition and creating cleaner sight lines. Consider removing extraneous stacks of books, piles of papers, and materials you are no longer using.

Create designated display areas for different types of information rather than spreading educational content randomly around the room. Having specific zones for word walls, math references, and current student work helps students know where to look for needed information without having to hunt for it. Empty picture frames mounted on walls create perfect organizational systems for rotating student work while maintaining a clean, gallery-like appearance.

Use the principles of good graphic design when creating displays. Limit color palettes to two or three complementary colors rather than using every bright marker in your collection. Choose simple, clean fonts that are easy to read from student seating areas.

Provide white space around essential information to make it stand out, rather than surrounding it with visual noise.

Establish systems for rotating displays based on the current curriculum. For example, when you're teaching science lessons about weather, weather-related displays take prominence while other content is stored away. This rotation keeps your walls current and purposeful while preventing information overload.

Consider which educational references students need displayed versus those that could be provided in individual folders or resource books. Sometimes, having materials that students can pull out when needed works better than having everything constantly visible on walls.

STEP 4: Create multiple regulation spaces within your classroom.

Design various options for students who need different types of sensory regulation throughout the day. Some students need quiet, low-stimulation spaces, while others benefit from areas where they can move and release energy. Having multiple options allows students to choose the support that best meets their current needs.

Design dedicated regulation areas that complement your portable regulation basket. Establish calm corners with soft seating, comfort items, and soothing activities that give students a proper place to settle and reset. For older students, calling it the Zen Den or Chill Space might make it more appealing.

Create movement-friendly areas as well. Some students regulate through physical activity, so having spaces where appropriate movement is welcomed can prevent problems before they start. This might include standing desks, exercise balls as seating options, or discreet movement tools like foot bands under desks. Offer flexible seating options so students can choose what is comfortable for them in the moment.

Design these regulation spaces to be naturally supervised without feeling monitored. Students should feel safe using these areas without worrying about being watched or judged. Position regulation spaces where you can provide support if needed, while still allowing students the privacy they need for emotional processing.

Teach students how to use these spaces appropriately and independently. Provide clear guidelines about when and how to access these areas, and model using them yourself when you need emotional breaks. Normalize the need for regulation rather than treating it as unusual or problematic.

STEP 5: **Add calming elements throughout your space.**

Incorporate natural elements, soft textures, and calming visuals that support self-regulation. You can add them over time by thoughtfully including items that promote peace and focus. You can find many of them for free or at a low cost by simply sharing a list of what you are looking for with students' families, as well as your family and friends.

Consider incorporating calming colors throughout your space. Soft blues, greens, and earth tones generally promote relaxation, while bright reds, yellows, and oranges increase stimulation and energy. Your classroom does not need to be boring, but you can choose colors intentionally based on their psychological effects. Start small, like exchanging the brightly colored containers on one shelf for neutral colored ones, or even baskets. Work toward unifying your storage, materials, and décor. You may even be able to paint a wall with coordinated hues.

STEP 6: **Address the acoustic environment and sound management.**

Develop a comprehensive approach to managing noise levels and sound quality in your classroom. When you think about the acoustic environment of your classroom, every surface and material matters. Rugs provide comfort and significantly reduce noise from chair movement and foot traffic. Curtains absorb sound while providing visual softness. Fabric wall hangings can serve dual purposes as art and sound-dampening. Be mindful of hygiene and allergy considerations when choosing soft materials.

Consider the acoustic needs of different activities, and plan accordingly. Story time might work better in a carpeted area with soft seating, while science experiments might be better suited for hard surfaces that are easy to clean. Having different acoustic zones allows for varied activities without overwhelming sensitive students.

Be aware of sounds from outside your classroom that might affect learning. Hallway noise, mechanical systems, and outdoor activities can all impact student focus and regulation. While you can't control all external sounds, you can plan activities around predictable noise and provide tools, such as noise-canceling headphones or earplugs, for students who need them.

OVERCOMING PUSHBACK

When you start creating calmer, less stimulating classroom environments, some colleagues, administrators, or parents may question whether you're providing enough rich learning experiences or worry that simpler spaces look unprofessional. Here's how to address common concerns while staying committed to creating environments that support all learners.

The classroom needs to be stimulating and engaging for learning. There's an essential difference between engaging and overwhelming. True engagement comes from students being able to focus on learning rather than being distracted by environmental chaos. When students can regulate their nervous systems in calm environments, they engage more deeply with content because their mental energy isn't being spent processing sensory overload.

You can point out that many high-performing educational systems around the world favor simpler, cleaner classroom designs that prioritize function over decoration. Student engagement should come from meaningful activities and relationships, not from sensory bombardment.

I need to display student work and educational resources. Absolutely, and creating calming environments doesn't mean eliminating all displays. It means being strategic about what you show, how you show it, and when you show it. Students benefit more from seeing their work displayed thoughtfully than from having every assignment compete for wall space simultaneously.

Consider rotating displays so current work gets prominence while older projects are stored in portfolios. Use simple, clean backgrounds that highlight student work without busy designs that overwhelm it. Create designated display areas rather than covering every available surface.

My principal expects classrooms to look a certain way. Many administrators are beginning to understand the importance of trauma-responsive environments and may be more receptive to changes than you expect. Explain how environmental modifications support student learning and regulation, focusing on the practical benefits you've observed. Document improvements in student behavior, focus, and engagement as a result.

Offer to pilot changes in your classroom while tracking student outcomes. Many administrators are willing to support approaches that improve student success, even if they initially seem unconventional. Frame environmental changes as evidence-based practices rather than personal preferences.

But I love decorating my classroom and making it cute! Creating beautiful learning environments and supporting students' regulation aren't mutually exclusive. You can have an attractive classroom that's also calming and functional. Focus your creative energy on thoughtful design choices that serve both aesthetic and functional purposes.

Consider channeling your decorating skills toward creating calming, beautiful spaces rather than busy, overwhelming ones. Natural elements, soft textures, and peaceful colors can be as visually appealing as bright bulletin boards, while being much more supportive of student needs.

My classroom is too dark without the fluorescent lights on. Start by experimenting with partial lighting solutions rather than turning off all overhead lights at once. Try turning off every other fluorescent bulb or just the lights in one section of your room. Maximize natural light by opening blinds and positioning key learning areas near windows. Add warm lamps or string lights to brighten specific areas without the harsh glare of institutional lighting. Our pupils dilate, and we can see just fine! What feels dark initially becomes cozy and focused once everyone adjusts to the softer lighting.

THE HACK IN ACTION

Mrs. Patel had always prided herself on having the most decorated classroom in her school. Every surface was covered with educational posters, student work, seasonal decorations, and motivational quotes. She spent hours creating elaborate bulletin boards and themed displays that changed monthly. Other teachers often complimented her Pinterest-worthy classroom.

But Mrs. Patel was puzzled by her students' behavior. Despite all her efforts to create an engaging environment, many students seemed distracted, anxious, and unable to focus for extended periods. Dante, a child from a migrant worker family who had experienced frequent moves, struggled to get through a whole day without asking to visit the nurse. Dante complained of headaches nearly every morning, developed stomachaches during independent work time, and often said he felt sick when the classroom got busy or loud. Mrs. Patel found herself writing nurse passes multiple times each day.

After attending a workshop on trauma-responsive practices, Mrs. Patel began to see her classroom through different eyes. She realized that what she thought was stimulating might be overwhelming for children whose bodies were already stressed. The constant visual input and harsh lighting might be contributing to Dante's physical symptoms rather than supporting his learning.

She decided to try an experiment. Over winter break, Mrs. Patel transformed her classroom. She took down most of the wall displays, leaving only current learning references that students used. She replaced bright, busy bulletin board borders with simple, neutral ones. She turned off the fluorescent lighting and brought in several lamps that provided warm, soft illumination.

Mrs. Patel added a small cozy corner with pillows and quiet activities, framing it as a place for rest and reflection rather than consequences. She introduced a few plants and created a small nature table with smooth stones and shells that students could touch for sensory input.

The transformation in her students was immediate and dramatic. Dante's daily complaints of headaches and stomachaches virtually disappeared. He stopped asking for nurse passes and began participating more actively in lessons. Students seemed more settled overall, and Mrs. Patel noticed that she felt more relaxed in the space as well.

Most surprisingly, academic engagement increased. Students could focus for longer periods and seemed less distracted during instruction. Behavioral incidents decreased significantly, and Mrs. Patel spent more time teaching and less time managing disruptions.

When colleagues asked about her "plain" classroom, Mrs. Patel explained how the environmental changes supported her students' learning and pointed to their improved engagement and behavior.

By spring, several other teachers had begun making similar modifications to their spaces.

Mrs. Patel learned that creating beautiful, effective learning environments doesn't require covering every surface with decorations. Sometimes, the most beautiful classroom is one where every child can feel calm, focused, and ready to learn.

When we create calming physical environments, we're not making our classrooms boring or unstimulating. We're making them accessible to every child's nervous system. We're designing spaces where students can focus on learning rather than spending mental energy processing environmental chaos.

This shift requires us to think about classroom design as a teaching tool. Every choice we make about lighting, visual displays, and sensory elements either supports student regulation or creates additional challenges for vulnerable learners.

The students who benefit the most from calming environments are often those who need our support the most. Many children who've experienced trauma, students with sensory processing differences, and kids dealing with stress at home struggle to learn effectively in overstimulating spaces. When we create environments that support their nervous systems, we're removing barriers to their success.

But here's the beautiful part: Calming environments benefit everyone. When classrooms feel peaceful and organized rather than chaotic and overwhelming, all students can focus better, regulate their emotions more effectively, and engage more deeply with the learning process.

Creating these supportive environments doesn't mean spending lots of money or completely redesigning your space. It means you're making thoughtful, intentional choices that prioritize students' well-being alongside academic goals. The most powerful changes can be the ones we take away instead of adding.

REFLECTION
QUESTIONS

1. **How does your current classroom environment impact students' nervous systems?** Consider whether your space feels calming and organized or busy and overwhelming from a student's perspective.

2. **What changes would have the biggest impact on creating a more regulation-supporting environment?** Look at lighting, visual clutter, noise levels, and sensory elements that might need an adjustment.

3. **How can you involve students in creating calming spaces that meet their needs?** Think about ways to gather student input about environmental modifications that would help them focus and feel comfortable.

4. **Which students might benefit the most from environmental modifications, and how can you support their specific sensory needs?** Consider individual students who seem overwhelmed, distracted, or dysregulated in your current space.

CONSTRUCT SPACES FOR SECURITY AND RISK-TAKING

Provide Consistent and Emotionally Safe Classrooms

Predictability brings about security.
— MAGDA GERBER, CHILD THERAPIST
AND INFANT SPECIALIST

NINE-YEAR-OLD AMARA HAD been in three different schools in two years, as her mother's military reassignment meant frequent moves. When Amara walked into Mrs. Kim's third-grade classroom for the first time, her eyes darted around the room, cataloging everything: Where was the teacher's desk? Which corner would be safest if she needed to hide? How quickly could she get to the door if needed? Her hands gripped her backpack straps like a lifeline.

Mrs. Kim noticed Amara's hypervigilant scanning and made a mental note. Over the next few days, she watched as Amara struggled during transitions, jumped whenever the schedule changed unexpectedly, and seemed to shut down completely when substitute teachers for the special classes appeared. Mrs. Kim realized that what may have looked like defiance or inattention was a trauma response to unpredictability.

But Mrs. Kim also noticed something else. Amara never raised her hand in math, even when she was working out problems correctly at her desk. During writing time, Amara would start sentences and then erase them rather than risk having the wrong answer. The classroom environment, while well-intentioned, had become a place where only perfect, right answers felt safe.

So, Mrs. Kim tried a different approach. She created a visual schedule that showed what they would do each day, including when transitions would happen and who might visit the classroom. She started modeling her own mistakes during lessons, saying things like, "Oops, I made an error. Let me think about this differently." Most importantly, she began celebrating wrong answers as "beautiful mistakes" that helped the whole class learn.

The transformation wasn't immediate, but it was remarkable. Slowly, Amara's shoulders began to relax. She started raising her hand during discussions, even when she wasn't sure of her answer. For the first time in years, Amara found a classroom that felt safe for learning because it offered both security and acceptance.

THE PROBLEM: WE'VE CREATED UNPREDICTABLE, RISK-AVERSE LEARNING ENVIRONMENTS

Let's be honest about a situation no one wants to admit. Schools are chaotic places, and it's not because anyone planned it that way.

Schedules change constantly due to assemblies, testing, and special events. Students are regularly pulled from class for various services, creating additional transitions and the awkwardness of being singled out when the intervention teacher arrives. Fire drills happen whenever the district decides. Substitute teachers appear with different rules and expectations. These disruptions aren't optional; they're necessary parts of running a school. But for many students, especially those who've experienced trauma, this constant unpredictability creates a recipe for dysregulation.

Children who have been in the foster care system face this challenge in an amplified way. It's trauma-*plus* in action: they've experienced the unpredictability of adults who were supposed to care for them but disappear, homes that promised permanence but turn out to be temporary, and safety that seemed guaranteed but proves to be an illusion. These students have learned that change often means loss, transitions can bring distress, and trusting new environments isn't safe. For them, whatever predictability we can create isn't a nice-to-have; it's neurologically necessary for learning to occur.

WE CLAIM TO VALUE THE LEARNING PROCESS, BUT OUR GRADING FOCUSES ON FINAL PRODUCTS. WE SAY MISTAKES HELP US LEARN, BUT THEN WE MARK THOSE MISTAKES AS FAILURES IN OUR GRADEBOOKS.

But here's where it gets worse. The age of accountability has layered another problem on top of this unavoidable unpredictability. We've created a deficit-focused, right-answer-obsessed educational culture that promotes fixed-mindset thinking, where students are terrified to make mistakes. Third-graders know they must pass reading tests to advance to fourth grade. High schoolers understand that wrong answers on standardized tests can determine their futures. The result? We're turning out students who are afraid to take risks.

When children become focused on avoiding mistakes instead of exploring ideas, their brains shift into "downstairs brain." They're in survival mode, trying to predict the right answer rather than thinking critically or creatively. This fear of being wrong has gotten so intense that many students won't raise their hands or participate in discussions. They freeze to avoid the risk of being incorrect, leading to a fixed-mindset belief that mistakes mean they're not smart, instead of mistakes helping their brains grow.

Think about the mixed messages we send. We say we want students to be creative and think critically, but we reward them for giving us the answers we expect. We contend that we encourage risk-taking and innovation, but our assessment systems penalize wrong answers. We claim to value the learning process, but our grading focuses on final products. We say mistakes help us learn, but then we mark those mistakes as failures in our gradebooks.

It feels like an impossible situation. Students are dealing with unpredictable school environments that keep their nervous systems on edge while simultaneously trying to perform perfectly on academic tasks where mistakes feel dangerous. It's like asking someone to solve complex problems while riding a roller coaster and judging them harshly for any errors.

Traditional responses make the situation worse. When students become dysregulated due to unpredictability or shut down due to a fear of mistakes, we often respond with isolation, time-outs, or removal from learning activities. For children affected by trauma, these responses trigger the abandonment fears their nervous systems are already primed to expect. Instead of helping them regulate and reengage, we're confirming their worst fears about relationships and safety.

The result is classrooms where students spend more mental

energy managing anxiety about what's coming next and whether they'll be right than they spend on the learning. Their brains are working overtime to predict threats and avoid mistakes instead of processing new information, making connections, and gaining understanding. We can't eliminate all the unpredictability that comes with running schools, but we can be much more intentional about creating the security and psychological safety that makes real learning possible.

THE HACK: CONSTRUCT SPACES FOR SECURITY AND RISK-TAKING

The solution isn't to create rigid, mistake-free classrooms where nothing ever changes. It's to design learning environments where predictability creates psychological safety, where mistakes are celebrated as learning opportunities, and where students know they can take intellectual risks without losing our care and support. When students know what to expect and they feel safe to be imperfect, their brains can shift from survival mode to learning mode.

This Hack requires us to think about predictability and psychological safety as learning tools, not limitations. Instead of viewing structure as the enemy of creativity and autonomy, we understand it as the foundation that makes creative risk-taking possible. Students can't think outside the box if they don't feel safe enough to explore what's inside it first.

The Core Strategy: Design Emotionally Safe, Structured Spaces with Developmentally Appropriate Expectations

The foundation of trauma-responsive classroom design is predictability that reduces anxiety while creating environments where mistakes become learning opportunities. This scenario means establishing consistent routines and expectations while explicitly teaching students that errors are valuable parts of the learning process.

Start by cultivating environments that balance safety and risk where mistakes are celebrated as essential to learning. Model your errors, share your thinking process when you get things wrong, and help students understand that their knowledge grows when they work through challenges and uncertainties.

Assemble a classroom community intentionally through relationships where you see your students as individuals, they feel safe with you, and they connect with each other. These tri-directional relationships create a safety net that allows for authentic risk-taking and genuine learning. Students need to feel known and valued as people, not just as academic performers.

Establish Consistent, Predictable Routines and Schedules

Learners thrive in environments that are familiar and consistent. Establish predictable routines that help students feel secure while front-loading necessary changes with adequate preparation and support. When students know what to expect, they can focus their mental energy on learning rather than trying to predict what's coming next.

Predictable routines are about creating the safety that allows flexibility and creativity to flourish. Understanding the daily patterns helps students successfully handle changes.

Create visual schedules or agendas that are accessible to all learners, including the students who need extra support. The schedules should include subjects and times, plus information about any visitors, special events, or changes to the routine. This visual device helps students feel prepared rather than surprised by their day.

Develop morning routines that help students transition smoothly from home to school, especially considering that many may be coming from chaotic or stressful home environments. The routines might include consistent greeting practices, chances for students to share information about their day, a morning meeting to discuss the agenda, and calming activities that help them feel ready to learn.

Design transition routines that prevent the chaos and dysregulation that often occur when moving between activities. Use consistent signals, provide adequate warning time, and create predictable procedures that students can follow independently. The goal is to make transitions feel manageable.

Model Taking Risks and Making Mistakes

A powerful way to create psychologically safe learning environments is to normalize mistake-making by modeling it yourself. When students see their teacher making errors, thinking through problems, and learning from mistakes, they understand that growth, not perfection, is the goal.

Say things like, "I'm not sure about this, so let me think out loud," or "Oops, I made an error. Let me figure out what went wrong and try again." This teaches students that uncertainty and errors are typical parts of learning.

When students make errors, respond with curiosity rather than correction. Ask questions like, "Can you explain your thinking when you tried that approach?" or "What can we learn from this mistake?" This curiosity helps students see errors as valuable information rather than evidence of inadequacy.

Create classroom language around mistakes that frames them positively and promotes a growth mindset. Some teachers use phrases like "beautiful mistakes," "learning moments," and "brain growth opportunities." The goal is to help students understand that real learning happens when they're working through challenges and uncertainties.

Provide Open-Ended Activities with Multiple Right Answers

Design learning experiences that allow for multiple correct responses, diverse approaches, and creative thinking. This practice reduces the anxiety that comes from trying to find the one right answer, and it encourages deeper thinking and authentic engagement.

Create math problems that can be solved in multiple ways, writing prompts that invite personal interpretation, and science investigations that lead to various discoveries. Shift from "What's the right answer?" to "Can you explain your thinking?"

> **WHEN STUDENTS SEE THAT THEIR CLASSMATES THINK DIFFERENTLY AND ALL CONTRIBUTE VALUABLE INSIGHTS, THEY BECOME MORE WILLING TO SHARE THEIR UNIQUE THINKING.**

Develop assessment approaches that value thinking processes over final answers. Use authentic documentation strategies, such as photos of student work, recorded conversations about their thinking, and portfolio collections, that show growth over time. Our students must understand that their learning journey matters more than their final destination.

Design collaborative activities that value and incorporate different perspectives and approaches. When students see that their classmates think differently and all contribute valuable insights, they become more willing to share their unique thinking.

Build Classroom Community Through Intentional Relationship Development

Create systematic opportunities to foster strong learning communities through mutual understanding: knowing your students as individuals, increasing their trust in you, and helping them connect with each other. These interconnected relationships enable authentic risk-taking and learning.

Implement consistent community circles or meetings where students can share experiences, celebrate each other's growth, and work through challenges together. These gatherings foster the relationships that make psychological safety possible while providing forums for addressing conflicts and celebrating successes.

Develop consistent ways to support each student's willingness to take academic risks and learn from mistakes, including individually checking in about their comfort with challenges, celebrating their brave thinking, or noting their growth in resilience. This work helps students feel seen as capable learners.

Model vulnerability around learning and mistake-making while maintaining appropriate boundaries. Find age-appropriate ways to share your experiences with taking academic risks, learning from errors, and growing through challenges. When students see you as someone who also makes mistakes and learns from them, they're more likely to trust you with their learning vulnerabilities.

Integrate Rhythm, Music, and Movement for Regulation

Use rhythmic activities, music, and movement to help students regulate their nervous systems and transition smoothly between activities. These tools are particularly powerful for children affected by trauma, whose regulation systems may need extra support.

Add rhythmic elements to transitions, cleanup times, and routine activities. These elements might include clapping patterns, singing familiar songs, or using rhythmic chants that help students move smoothly from one activity to another while staying regulated.

Incorporate movement breaks and regulation activities throughout the day, especially before challenging academic tasks or after high-energy activities. Stretches, breathing exercises, and movement games can help students feel calm and focused, ready for learning.

Use music strategically to create calming environments, signal transitions, or enhance learning activities. Different types of music can support regulation needs, from calming anxious students to energizing tired learners.

WHAT **YOU** CAN DO TOMORROW

Ready to start creating more predictable, psychologically and emotionally safe learning environments? These immediate changes can help your students feel more secure and ready to take academic risks. You can implement these ideas right away, or you can start with the ones that feel most natural to your teaching style.

- **Start a consistent morning routine tomorrow: backpacks, materials, and one simple starting activity in the same order every day.** Create a predictable pattern that students can count on. Maybe backpacks go in the same place, they get out the same materials, and start with the same type of warm-up activity. For middle and high school, this might be entering quietly, checking the board for today's agenda, and starting with a consistent bell-ringer or journal prompt. Keep it simple, but make it the same sequence every day.

- **Ask, "Can you explain your thinking?" when students make an error (instead of only correcting them).** This phrase shift transforms mistakes from failures into learning opportunities. When students explain their reasoning, you can understand their thinking process *and* they learn that their thought processes matter, not just their final answers.

- **Reduce one unnecessary transition and create a longer activity block.** Look at your schedule and find one time when you're switching activities that could be combined or extended. Maybe reading and writing can flow together, or morning work can connect directly to your first subject. Fewer transitions means more time for deep learning.

- **Add rhythm to one transition or activity.** Choose a daily routine like cleanup time, lining up, or moving to the carpet, and add a rhythmic element like a clapping pattern, familiar song, or chant. An alternative for older students might be playing the same background music during independent work time, using a consistent verbal countdown pattern, or adding a rhythmic timer sound for activity transitions. Students find rhythm naturally regulating, and it makes transitions feel predictable and calm.

- **Give students a preview of tomorrow's schedule before they leave today.** Let them know what to expect, including any changes from the usual routine, special visitors, or activities that might be different. Even small previews like, "Tomorrow, we'll start with our usual morning routine, then math, reading, and we have art instead of music," help students feel prepared and not surprised.

A BLUEPRINT FOR FULL IMPLEMENTATION

Creating predictable and psychologically safe learning environments requires systematic attention to routines, relationships, academic design, and regulation support. You're building a foundation that allows for supported flexibility, authentic learning, and growth-mindset development.

STEP 1: Create comprehensive predictability systems.

Post detailed visual schedules and agendas that go beyond basic subject listings to include advance notice of any changes, visitor information, and transitions. Develop consistent response patterns for common classroom situations so students can predict how you'll handle mistakes, conflicts, and celebrations.

Ensure substitute teacher plans maintain classroom routines and predictability as much as possible. Include detailed information about individual students who may need extra support during changes, classroom procedures that help maintain consistency, and activities that don't require navigating complex new systems.

Design backup plans for when unexpected changes occur. What happens if assemblies get canceled? How do you handle technology failures or schedule disruptions? Having consistent protocols for managing change can help maintain emotional safety when circumstances shift unexpectedly.

Establish clear communication systems with students, families, and caregivers about upcoming changes. The more significant the change, the more advance notice and preparation students need in order to handle it successfully while maintaining their sense of security and readiness to learn.

STEP 2: **Transform assessment and documentation that values process over product and promotes a growth mindset.**

Transform your assessment practices to focus on thinking, problem-solving, and growth over time rather than final answers or products in the moment. Create rubrics that celebrate children's reasoning, creative thinking, persistence through challenges, and learning from mistakes.

Develop portfolio systems that document students' learning journeys, including their mistakes, evolution of problem-solving, and growth in risk-taking over time. Use photos of student work, recorded conversations about their thought processes, and reflective writings that reveal how students understand their learning and cognitive development.

Create documentation that captures risk-taking and mistake-making as evidence of learning. (Older students can help create the documentation.) When students see their errors and explorations valued and documented, they understand that a growth mindset isn't just a concept we talk about but one we measure and celebrate.

Design assessment approaches that help students develop a metacognitive awareness of their learning processes through reflection journals, goal tracking, and self-assessment conversations. This work might include reflection journals where students track their thinking, learning conferences where they discuss their growth, or portfolio reflections that help them see their progress. Teach them to recognize when their brains are growing, when they're taking appropriate intellectual risks, and how to reflect on their learning strategies and progress using tools like exit tickets that ask about their thinking processes.

STEP 3: Cultivate caregiver and community understanding of growth mindsets and mistake-friendly learning.

Develop clear communication strategies that help caregivers understand why mistakes are celebrated in your classroom and how this approach accelerates learning. Share ongoing information about growth mindsets and brain plasticity in family-friendly language.

Create opportunities for families to understand the difference between emotional safety and low expectations and how their children can be challenged and supported simultaneously. Many families need to understand that growth-mindset environments better prepare students for future challenges.

Establish home-school partnerships around growth-mindset development by providing families and caregivers with language and strategies they can use at home to reinforce mistake-friendly learning, which is especially important since it is so different from the way many of them learned. Share phrases like "Your brain just grew!" and "What did you learn from that mistake?" that families can use during homework time, creating consistency between home and school.

Design family engagement activities that demonstrate growth-mindset principles in action, such as family learning nights where parents and students work through challenging problems together. Instead of traditional parent-teacher conferences, invite families to join you for student-led conferences where their child presents their learning journeys, including mistakes and growth, beyond their final products.

STEP 4: Optimize scheduling and pacing to meet learners' needs.

Systematically examine your daily schedule to reduce unnecessary transitions while creating longer integrated learning blocks that honor how children learn and develop. Our brains need time to process, explore, and make connections, and finding this time can be a challenge when they constantly switch between subjects and activities.

Create flexible scheduling options that allow for extended engagement when learning is flowing well and additional processing time when students need it. It might mean combining related subjects into longer blocks or designing project times that integrate multiple content areas naturally. In older grades that use departmentalized teaching, multiple educators can identify natural overlaps in content and work together to co-design units around shared themes or topics. When possible, align subjects with similar energies to be back-to-back to maintain mental flow and avoid cognitive whiplash.

Insert adequate transition time between activities so students don't feel rushed or anxious about moving to the next task. Include brief regulation moments, reflection time, or organizational activities that help students feel prepared and calm. For students who switch classes often, designate the first few minutes in your room as a settling in period, with time for independent work, journaling, or check-ins, and the last few minutes for reflection.

Design learning experiences that allow for natural pacing, not artificial time constraints driven by schedules over learning needs. If you teach in an environment with short class periods, advocate for a block schedule, where students have fewer, and longer, classes a day. Or work with your colleagues and administrators to add a flex schedule where students can revisit the class of their choice to continue working on assignments and projects once or twice a week. When students can work at appropriate speeds without feeling rushed, they experience less stress and produce higher-quality thinking and work.

STEP 5: Empower students through self-advocacy and metacognition skills development.

Teach students to recognize their own learning patterns, regulation needs, and optimal conditions for risk-taking and growth. Help them understand how their brains work best and how to advocate for the support they need to be successful learners.

Encourage students to request predictability supports when needed, whether that's advance notice about changes, extra processing time, or clarification about expectations. Students who understand their needs can become partners in creating optimal learning conditions.

Help students develop metacognitive awareness of their mistake-making, risk-taking, and learning processes through modeling, think-alouds, sentence stems, and age-appropriate vocabulary to describe "thinking about thinking." Teach them to recognize when they're growing, when they're taking appropriate intellectual risks, and how their brains respond to different types of challenges and support.

Create opportunities for students to share their learning strategies and growth-mindset discoveries with classmates, designing a classroom culture where everyone becomes an expert in understanding how learning happens and how brains grow through challenge and effort.

STEP 6: Develop and sustain ongoing reflection and adjustment systems.

Develop regular assessment protocols for evaluating classroom psychological safety, predictability effectiveness, and growth-mindset development. You might include student surveys about their comfort with risk-taking, observation data about participation patterns, and documentation of mistake-making frequency and student responses.

Create student feedback mechanisms, such as exit tickets, that help you understand which predictability supports are most helpful and which growth-mindset strategies resonate the most with different learners. Students often have insights about their learning needs that can guide your continued refinement of classroom systems.

Ensure reflection practices help you notice your responses to student mistakes, risk-taking, and learning processes. The most effective mistake-friendly classrooms are led by teachers who model a growth mindset by examining their own thinking patterns.

Establish systems for sharing successful strategies with colleagues and learning from other educators who are implementing similar approaches. Growth-mindset and emotional-safety practices can be improved through collaboration and shared problem-solving.

OVERCOMING PUSHBACK

When you start creating more predictable, mistake-friendly learning environments, some colleagues, administrators, and parents may worry about academic rigor or preparation for standardized testing. Here's how to address common concerns while staying committed to providing emotional safety that enhances learning.

How do I assess if there are multiple right answers? Focus on documenting student thinking processes, growth over time, and problem-solving approaches beyond just capturing the final answers. Use portfolios, photos of student work, recorded conversations, and observation notes to capture learning that standardized assessments miss. When students can explain their thinking and show growth in their reasoning, that's evidence of real learning happening. Share examples of how process-focused assessment provides more useful information about student understanding than answer-focused grading. When you can see how students think through problems, you can provide much more targeted and effective instruction.

Our curriculum is focused on finding the right answer, and I have to prepare students for standardized tests. Find ways to modify existing activities to be more open-ended. Turn worksheet problems into games or investigation opportunities, add "explain your thinking" components to assignments, and create multiple pathways for students to approach the required content. Even when a question has one correct answer, emphasize that there are multiple ways to get there, and value the different problem-solving approaches students use. Help colleagues understand that students who feel safe to think, explore, and make mistakes perform better on assessments because they've developed a deeper understanding and stronger problem-solving skill set.

I don't have time for community-building when we have so much curriculum to cover. Integrate relationship-building into academic content. Use math problems that connect to student interests, create writing assignments that include personal sharing, and design science investigations that encourage collaboration and discussion. Share information about how much instructional time is lost to behavior problems, anxiety, and disengagement when students don't feel safe and connected. The time invested in developing a sense of community pays dividends in increased focus, cooperation, and learning.

Students need to learn to handle pressure and unpredictability because that's what the real world is like. Predictable, supportive learning environments better prepare students for handling challenges because they develop strong internal regulation skills and confidence in their ability to learn and grow. Students who feel secure are much more resilient when facing difficulties. Explain that we can gradually increase students' capacity to handle uncertainty and pressure while maintaining the emotional safety they need to develop these skills. It's like learning to drive in an empty parking lot before navigating busy highways.

THE HACK IN ACTION

Mr. Hamilton's fourth-grade classroom felt like a pressure cooker. Students seemed paralyzed by perfectionism, refusing to participate in discussions unless they were absolutely certain of their answers. Math time had become particularly painful, as children would erase their work repeatedly rather than risk showing incorrect thinking. The few students who did raise their hands were always the same ones, while others had given up on engaging altogether.

The breaking point came during a science lesson when Mr. Hamilton asked students to hypothesize about what would happen in an experiment. Dead silence. Finally, one brave student whispered, "I don't want to be wrong." That's when Mr. Hamilton realized the classroom culture was working against learning rather than supporting it.

The transformation began when Mr. Hamilton changed how mistakes were handled. He focused on building a culture where wrong answers were treasured. He started collecting "beautiful mistakes" on a special bulletin board, celebrating errors that led to new insights and understanding. During lessons, Mr. Hamilton would deliberately make thinking errors and openly model how to work through confusion.

Most importantly, he redesigned activities to have multiple correct approaches. Math problems became investigations with various solution paths. Writing prompts encouraged personal interpretation rather than seeking teacher-approved responses. Science experiments focused on observation and wondering rather than getting predetermined results.

The shift was remarkable. Students who had been silent for months began raising their hands tentatively, then with growing confidence. Discussion quality improved dramatically as children shared their diverse thinking instead of parroting expected answers. Even mistakes became celebrations, as students learned to say, "I disagree because …" and "That's interesting, but what if …"

Destiny, a student who had experienced multiple school changes due to housing instability, showed the most dramatic improvement. Previously, she had been reluctant to participate and seemed to shut down whenever she felt uncertain about answers. With a mistake-friendly environment that celebrated diverse thinking, Destiny began raising her hand during discussions, taking creative risks in her writing, and even helping other students when they felt confused or frustrated.

By spring, the classroom buzzed with intellectual risk-taking. Students would volunteer to share incorrect solutions to help classmates learn, and authentic curiosity had replaced performance anxiety. Mr. Hamilton had created exactly what he'd hoped for—a space where security and risk-taking could coexist.

When we design predictable spaces that celebrate mistakes as learning opportunities, we're not limiting academic growth; we're creating the conditions that make real learning possible. Students whose nervous systems are constantly activated by unpredictability and the fear of being wrong simply cannot access the parts of their brains responsible for complex thinking, creative problem-solving, and meaningful risk-taking.

This shift requires us to understand that predictability and psychological safety aren't enemies of rigor but foundations for it. When students know what to expect and feel safe to be imperfect, they can focus their mental energy on learning, simultaneously relieving their anxiety. They can take intellectual risks because they feel emotionally supported.

The students who benefit the most from predictable, mistake-friendly environments are often those who need our support the most. Students who've experienced trauma, children who've been in the foster care system who've learned that change often brings loss, and children whose perfectionist tendencies mask deep insecurities all desperately need classrooms that feel stable and accepting of human imperfection.

But predictable, psychologically safe environments don't just help vulnerable students. They support every learner by reducing anxiety, increasing the willingness to take intellectual risks, and creating the emotional foundation that allows for authentic engagement and creative thinking. When we design spaces where students know what to expect and feel safe to make mistakes, we give them the greatest gift possible—the freedom to think, explore, and grow.

REFLECTION
QUESTIONS

1. **How predictable is your classroom environment?** Consider schedules, routines, and responses from a student's perspective.

2. **Where can you create more opportunities for safe risk-taking?** Think about activities that currently feel high-stakes and how you might redesign them to encourage exploration and mistake-making.

3. **How do you currently respond to student mistakes, and what message does that send about learning?** Consider both your words and your body language when students make errors.

4. **Which students might be most affected by unpredictability or the fear of making mistakes?** Often, these are students who seem anxious, perfectionistic, or reluctant to participate in discussions.

HACK 7

INTEGRATE REGULATION SUPPORT THROUGHOUT THE DAY

Develop Brain-Ready Learners Through Co-Regulation

If the child is too dysregulated, they will not be open to any new learning or experience. And if you continue to expect the child to pay attention, focus, and learn, you will be eroding the child's sense of safety with you.
— DR. BRUCE PERRY, TRAUMA SPECIALIST

Zara sits in the back corner of her seventh-grade English class, her hoodie pulled up despite the warm classroom. Her leg bounces rhythmically under the desk as she stares at the blank page in front of her. The creative writing assignment should be engaging. She is supposed to write about a place that feels safe, but Zara's mind keeps racing to this morning's argument with her mom about chores. When her teacher, Mr. Nistler, approaches to offer encouragement, Zara snaps, "I can't do this stupid assignment!" and shoves her notebook onto the floor.

Mr. Nistler pauses. Six months ago, he would have sent Zara to the office for disruption and defiance. He might have assigned detention or extra homework. But now, he recognizes what he's seeing—a dysregulated nervous system trying desperately to feel safe. Instead of consequences, Zara needs co-regulation.

"It sounds like you're pretty overwhelmed right now," Mr. Nistler says quietly, maintaining a respectful distance while keeping his voice calm and steady. "Would it help to take some deep breaths together, or would you rather have a few minutes to reset in the Chill Space?"

Zara's shoulders relax slightly at his nonthreatening tone and distance. She's been in survival mode since breakfast, and her system is finally recognizing safety. "I don't know how to write about safe places," she whispers. "I don't think I have any."

Mr. Nistler sits at her eye level, his presence steady and reassuring. "That makes perfect sense. How about we start with a different topic? Maybe you could write about a place where you'd like to feel safe, or even what safety might feel like in your body." He gently taps his pen against his leg in a slow, steady rhythm, giving Zara's nervous system a calming pattern to focus on while she processes her emotions.

This shift—from managing behavior to supporting regulation— changes everything.

THE PROBLEM: WE'RE TRYING TO EDUCATE BEFORE WE REGULATE

A fundamental disconnect exists in education today: we're expecting learning from dysregulated brains.

We ask students to solve complex problems when their brains are stuck in survival mode. We expect them to remember yesterday's lesson when their stress response systems are activated. We demand focus and attention from minds that are scanning for danger and are too busy to process information. It's like asking a surgeon to perform brain surgery while being chased by a bear.

The disconnect is in how we respond when students *can't* meet those expectations. Instead of recognizing when children are dysregulated, we often interpret their struggles as defiance, laziness, or a lack of motivation. We increase consequences, raise our voices, and remove students from the class, further exacerbating the dysregulation.

Yet, we continue to operate as if regulation and learning are separate issues.

Consider the student who arrives at school after a chaotic morning at home, having witnessed an argument between caregivers or overslept and missed breakfast. The student's cortisol levels are elevated, the sympathetic nervous system is activated, and the brain is primed for survival rather than learning. When we immediately launch into instruction, we're setting up this student for failure.

For students who have experienced trauma, the expectation to learn while in dysregulation is particularly harmful. Their stress response systems are often hypervigilant, interpreting neutral situations as threatening. A surprise quiz becomes a threat. A change in routine triggers anxiety. A raised voice activates their fight, flight, freeze, or fawn response. Traditional approaches—demanding compliance, using consequences, and removing students from instruction—can escalate situations when these children need support instead.

Imagine children in foster care who are experiencing trauma-*plus*, the added trauma caused by being in an out-of-home situation that is *on top of* their original trauma. When we expect immediate academic engagement from children whose entire world feels unstable, we're asking them to perform an extraordinarily challenging task.

The result is a cycle where dysregulated students continue to struggle academically and behaviorally, teachers become frustrated trying to teach unreachable brains, and classroom environments become tense. We wonder why our most challenging students aren't making progress, not realizing that we're asking the impossible: academic performance from brains that aren't biologically ready to learn.

THE HACK: INTEGRATE REGULATION SUPPORT THROUGHOUT THE DAY

Educators don't have to choose between academic rigor and emotional support. Regulation enables learning without competing with it. When we help students feel calm and safe, we're not taking away from instruction time—we're making instruction possible.

This Hack requires us to shift from reactive crisis management to proactive regulation support. Instead of waiting for dysregulation to disrupt learning, we weave regulation into the fabric of our classroom routines and interactions.

The Core Strategy: Use Co-Regulation to Support Brain-Ready Learning

Co-regulation is the practice of using your calm, regulated nervous system to help students return to a peaceful state where learning is possible. Rather than expecting your students to self-regulate when they are struggling, *you* become the external regulator who helps them get centered again. This process means staying emotionally steady during student crises, matching their energy levels before gradually bringing the energy down, and creating predictable regulation opportunities throughout the day that prevent dysregulation.

Unlike self-help strategies that require students to think their way out of emotional states, co-regulation works with the body's natural tendency to sync with others. When we stay calm in the presence of chaos, we become a stabilizing force.

Co-Regulate Across the Grades

This approach works for all students because it's based on how human beings are wired. Kindergartners and high schoolers alike have internal systems that respond to safety cues from trusted adults. The specific strategies may look different across age groups. A five-year-old might benefit from simpler language and more concrete visual cues, while a fifteen-year-old may prefer understanding the science behind what's happening and having more autonomy in choosing regulation tools. But the underlying principle remains the same.

For younger students, regulation support might be more visible and direct. We might lead breathing exercises, offer comfort items, or create dedicated calm-down spaces. Teaching children how to recognize and identify different feelings and emotions, and helping them verbalize what their bodies need to feel safe and ready to learn, are foundational concepts to support their emotional development.

With older students, regulation support becomes more subtle, but no less valuable. We might begin class with brief mindfulness moments, teach stress management techniques, or model staying calm under pressure. We respect their growing independence while still providing the co-regulation that adolescent brains desperately need during this period of intense development.

The key is integration. Regulation isn't an add-on to the curriculum—it's the foundation that makes the curriculum accessible. When we weave brief regulation activities throughout the day, we're investing in the brain state that makes learning possible.

WHAT **YOU** CAN DO TOMORROW

Ready to start supporting regulation in your classroom? You can implement these strategies immediately while you work toward more comprehensive changes.

- **Start the day with a brief, predictable regulation routine.** It might include a few minutes of deep breathing or gentle movement integrated into the existing morning meeting to create a mindful transition from home to school. Older students can benefit from an open-ended mindfulness question, a brief check-in activity, or calming music as they enter your classroom. Middle and high school students may initially resist any routines that feel childish, but they often appreciate transitions from hallway chaos to focused learning time.

- **Practice a co-regulation technique appropriate for your students.** For elementary students, direct approaches can provide clear, immediate support. These techniques include sitting near a dysregulated child to be in close proximity, matching the student's energy level before gradually bringing it down, taking deep breaths, naming and validating their feelings, and modeling calm body language. For older students, focus on being nearby without crowding, using a consistently calm voice, and offering choices for regulation strategies. Adolescents need to maintain dignity while receiving support, so your co-regulation might look like quietly offering options rather than directing specific actions.

- **Add a few regulation breaks into your existing schedule.** No major schedule restructuring required. Add thirty seconds of deep breathing before transitions, gentle stretches between subjects, or brief movement breaks when you notice energy levels dropping. You'll quickly see how these small investments in regulation pay dividends in focus and engagement.

- **Play games that teach kids to pause, think, and act.** Games that encourage impulse control and focus include *Simon Says*, *Red Light Green Light*, *Duck Duck Goose,* and the *Freeze Song.* The classic improv game *Two-Headed Monster* has a duo of students collaborate to tell a story. The catch is that each "monster" must alternate speaking one word at a time. Students can engage in an indoor snowball fight by writing kind words about a classmate on a piece of paper, crumpling it up, and waiting until a countdown ends to throw it. After the battle is complete, each child picks up a paper snowball, opens it, and reads the positive messages aloud. Board games can also help children practice turn-taking and managing a range of emotions, from excitement when winning to frustration when losing, both of which help students improve their regulation skills.

- **Stream music to affect the mood and energy of the class.** Music can be incredibly regulating, and the beats per minute, or tempo, can influence your students' emotional and cognitive responses. Slower-tempo music (40–60 bpm) helps to reduce the heart rate and encourages relaxation and calm, while faster tempos (100–160+ bpm) elevate heart rates and often energize students. Music at 60–80 bpm is particularly comforting because it mimics the mother's heartbeat that children hear in the womb, providing a familiar rhythm that is naturally soothing. Use this moderate tempo as background music during work times to promote focus. Be sure to offer earplugs or noise-canceling headphones for those who have difficulty concentrating and need a quieter environment. Or, if students have individual devices, let them use headphones to listen to the music that is right for them at that moment.

A BLUEPRINT FOR FULL IMPLEMENTATION

STEP 1: Learn to recognize dysregulation signs across age levels.

Understanding what dysregulation looks like at different ages helps you respond appropriately without taking behaviors personally or assuming defiance. Dysregulation rarely looks like obvious distress. More often, it appears as behaviors we might label as defiant, lazy, or attention-seeking.

For younger students, dysregulation often appears as hyper-activity, emotional meltdowns, withdrawal, aggression, or difficulty following familiar routines. A kindergartner who typically follows directions easily but suddenly can't remember classroom procedures is likely struggling emotionally, not being defiant. You might also notice increased clumsiness, regression in skills they've mastered, excessive silliness, or an inability to transition between activities. Some children become overly compliant when overwhelmed, appearing fine on the surface while their internal systems are highly stressed.

Physical signs in young children include rapid breathing, fidgeting that seems beyond their control, difficulty making eye contact, or covering their ears frequently. Watch for children who seem spacey or disconnected, as this freeze response is often missed because it doesn't disrupt the classroom.

Dysregulation looks different in older children. You might see mood swings, social drama escalation, academic shutdown, increased conflicts with peers, or extreme perfectionism alternating with complete avoidance. A typically engaged eighth-grader who suddenly refuses to participate may be overwhelmed, not oppositional. Middle schoolers might become argumentative about small details, struggle with decision-making, or show dramatic changes in their friend groups.

Look for shifts in academic patterns: the student who usually completes homework but suddenly has a string of missing assignments, the child who typically participates but becomes silent for days, or the learner who shifts from careful work to careless mistakes. These changes often indicate internal stress.

High school students often show dysregulation through anxiety symptoms, withdrawal from social connections, risky behaviors, or all-or-nothing thinking about academics and relationships. Remember that adolescent brains are still developing, making regulation particularly challenging during these years. You might notice increased absences, dramatic changes in appearance or friend groups, extreme reactions to feedback, or difficulty managing multiple deadlines.

Create documentation systems to track patterns and trends. Notice what times of day, activities, or environmental factors seem to trigger dysregulation for individual students. Keep a brief log, noting: What happened before the dysregulation? What did it look like? How long did it last? What helped the student return to baseline? This information becomes invaluable for moving beyond responding to problems to preventing problems.

Consider environmental factors that contribute to dysregulation. Is it often after lunch? Before tests? When the schedule changes? During group work? Understanding these patterns helps you provide proactive support rather than reactive consequences.

STEP 2: Build comprehensive regulation toolkits.

Expand on the calming physical environments we discussed in Hack 5 by developing specific resources for regulation support. Think of this work as creating a regulation toolkit where different students can access what their individual nervous systems need to return to calm.

For younger students, actively guide them to the regulation tools in your physical environment (from Hack 5) during moments when they need support. Teach students when and how to use stress balls or fidgets by modeling their use during your moments of stress. Introduce weighted lap pads or soft blankets during predictable challenging times, like before tests or after recess transitions. Practice using comfort items together during calm moments so students know they're available during difficult ones. Lead movement routines from yoga cards or dancing scarves as whole-class regulation breaks, then encourage individual students to access them independently. Guide students through visual breathing prompts rather than expecting them to use these tools intuitively, showing them how your breathing slows when you're feeling overwhelmed.

Create calm-down kits that travel with students who need them in other classes. Include items like noise-canceling headphones, sunglasses for light sensitivity, small materials for tactile stimulation, and laminated cards with breathing exercises. Some children benefit from oral motor input, so consider safe chewable items or sugar-free gum for older elementary students.

For older students, focus on more mature but equally effective tools. Discrete fidgets that don't draw peer attention work well. Think stress rings, textured strips that attach under desks, or small objects that fit in pockets. Help students download breathing apps they can access independently, such as guided meditation programs or breathing pattern apps with visual cues.

Encourage older students to create calming or energizing music playlists they can access during designated times, or invite them to help you create a school-appropriate class playlist. Beyond music, provide multiple ways for students to process their emotions independently. Journaling options for processing emotions might include prompted notebooks, sketchbooks, and voice memo apps for students who prefer verbal processing.

High school students benefit from stress management apps, meditation resources, and information about building peer support systems. Help them understand that regulation tools aren't signs of weakness but evidence of emotional intelligence and self-awareness. Teach them about the connection between physical wellness and emotional regulation and how sleep, nutrition, and exercise impact their ability to manage stress.

Remember that individual students may need specific accommodations. Some children regulate through movement, and others through quiet withdrawal. Some need more sensory input, and others need less. Adding variety to your toolkit ensures you can meet diverse needs. What works for one student might overwhelm another, so having options allows for personalized regulation support.

Consider cultural factors as well. Some students may come from backgrounds where emotional expression is handled differently, and regulation tools need to respect these differences while still providing support. Always ask students what helps them feel calm rather than assuming what should work.

STEP 3: Establish consistent, predictable regulation routines.

Create predictable opportunities for regulation throughout your day, adapting the approach to your students' developmental needs.

The key is consistency. Students benefit from knowing what to expect and when to expect it, allowing their stress response systems to be prepared.

THE GOAL IS TO MAKE REGULATION SUPPORT SO NATURAL THAT IT BECOMES A PART OF LEARNING RATHER THAN SEPARATE FROM IT.

Morning circle times that include brief check-ins work exceptionally well for younger children. Start with questions like, "How is your body feeling today?" or "What color is your energy right now?" Use visual supports such as weather metaphors—sunny, cloudy, stormy—to help children identify their internal states.

Transition songs can help with shifts between activities and serve dual purposes. They signal upcoming changes, which reduces anxiety and provides rhythmic regulation through music and movement. When you use the same song consistently for a specific transition, students begin to anticipate what's coming next. This predictability helps them mentally and emotionally prepare for the change.

Scheduled movement breaks throughout the day can prevent dysregulation from occurring in the first place. This movement might include stretches, brain breaks with specific actions, and walking as a class to the library or other space within the school when you notice energy levels rising. Establish predictable times throughout the day when all students can access regulation support. The goal is to make regulation support so natural that it becomes a part of learning rather than separate from it. Consider the rhythm of your school day when planning regulation routines. Many students need support after lunch, before challenging assessments, during transition times, or at the end of long days. Build brief regulation moments into these naturally challenging times.

For older students, brief mindfulness moments at the beginning of class signal that emotional awareness is valued and normal. You might include thirty seconds of focused breathing, a quick gratitude share, or a moment to notice how they're feeling as they enter your space. Add stress-check surveys that they can complete independently—either on paper or digitally—to allow students to communicate their needs without having to verbalize them publicly. The goal is to create a way for students to advocate for their regulation needs before small problems become big ones.

Middle schoolers particularly benefit from understanding that emotional ups and downs are standard parts of development. Create peer-regulation partnerships where students can support each other's emotional wellness. Teach them that checking in with friends about stress levels is a sign of maturity.

High school students need to develop individual regulation plans that will serve them beyond the classroom. Help them identify their personal stress signals, discover which regulation strategies work best for them, and practice advocating for their needs. Provide access to stress management workshops or resources, and integrate mental health awareness into academic content when appropriate.

Make these routines optional but consistent for all grade levels. Some students will need to observe before participating, while others may prefer their own version of the activity. Either way, you can create a classroom culture where emotional awareness and regulation are valued parts of learning.

STEP 4: Teach about emotions and regulation at appropriate levels.

Help students understand their emotional experiences and develop a vocabulary for communicating their needs. This process empowers students to cease being passive recipients of adult support and start being partners in their regulation.

Emphasize the analogies introduced in earlier chapters with younger students. The "upstairs brain" for thinking and the "downstairs brain" for big emotions help children understand why they sometimes feel overwhelmed. Use feeling charts with photographs of faces or emojis to help them identify and communicate their emotional states. Adding a mirror can provide immediate visual feedback to children who need extra support. Teach feeling identification through stories, role-play, and frequent modeling throughout the day. Read books where characters experience different emotions and discuss how feelings show up in bodies and behaviors.

Cultivate an emotional vocabulary that goes beyond happy, sad, mad, and scared. Introduce words like frustrated, disappointed, excited, worried, proud, and embarrassed. Use emotion wheels or thermometers that help children identify what they're feeling and how intensely they're feeling it. Practice emotion recognition during calm moments so students can access the skills during challenging times.

Help all students understand that all feelings are okay, but we can choose how we respond to them. Use language like, "Your anger makes sense, and let's find a safe way to express it" rather than "Don't be angry." Model your own emotion regulation through think-alouds, stating, "I notice I'm feeling frustrated right now because the document camera isn't working. I'm going to take three deep breaths and then ask for help."

Introduce age-appropriate information to tweens and teens about adolescent brain development and why emotional intensity increases during these years. Middle schoolers often feel relief when they learn that their emotional experiences are normal and biological rather than signs of personal weakness. Explain how stress affects learning and decision-making, helping them understand why regulation skills matter for academic success.

Teach older students about the connection between physical health and emotional regulation. Discuss how sleep, nutrition, exercise, and screen time impact their ability to manage stress and emotions. Help them identify their personal stress signals, such as tight shoulders, racing thoughts, and irritability, so they can intervene before reaching crisis points.

High school students can engage with more sophisticated concepts about emotional intelligence as a life skill. Discuss how regulation abilities impact relationships, work performance, and overall life satisfaction. Help them understand that developing these skills now will serve them beyond your classroom and throughout their lives.

Normalize the need for regulation support rather than treating it as unusual or problematic. Use language that frames regulation breaks as wise choices, such as, "It looks like your brain needs a reset. What would help you feel ready to learn again?"

This approach teaches students that regulation is a skill to develop rather than a failure to hide.

STEP 5: Practice age-appropriate co-regulation techniques.

Master the art of using your calm presence to help students return to regulated states. Co-regulation is a powerful tool in your regulation toolkit, and it requires practice and deliberate intent to implement effectively.

For younger students, co-regulation often involves direct physical proximity when safe and appropriate. Position yourself at the student's eye level by sitting or kneeling rather than standing over them. Use slow, deliberate movements that signal safety rather than urgency. Practice breathing together during challenging moments, making your breathing visible and audible so the child can match your rhythm. Your calm presence helps them regulate and return to baseline.

Use a consistently calm voice, even when students are escalated. Aim for steady and reassuring, not monotone and emotionless. Avoid rapid speech or high-pitched tones that can increase anxiety. Instead, speak slowly and use simple language: "You're safe here. I'm going to stay with you. We can figure this out together."

Physical co-regulation for younger students might include offering appropriate comfort such as a gentle hand on the shoulder, sitting close by, or a weighted lap pad. Always ask permission before physical contact and respect students' responses. Some children find touch overwhelming when dysregulated, while others crave the connection.

For older students, co-regulation looks like offering a respectful distance while remaining emotionally available. Middle and high school students need to maintain dignity while receiving support, so your co-regulation might be less physically obvious but equally essential. Position yourself nearby without crowding, maintain open body language, and resist the urge to immediately fix or solve their problems.

Practice coaching students through difficult situations. Reflect what you observe without judgment by saying things like, "I can see you're frustrated right now," or "This seems overwhelming." Validate their experience before moving to problem-solving with phrases such as, "That sounds really challenging," or "I can understand why you'd feel upset about that."

Offer choices for regulation strategies. "Would it help to take some deep breaths, or would you prefer a few minutes of quiet time?" This approach honors their developing autonomy while still providing support. Adolescents especially need to feel they have some control over their regulation process.

For all ages, remember that co-regulation aims to provide a safe relationship where students can experience and process difficult feelings. Sometimes, the most powerful co-regulation is simply staying calm and present while a student works through their emotions. For children who have been in the foster care system especially, consistent co-regulation from a trusted adult can be transformative, as many have rarely experienced reliable emotional support from caregivers.

Practice staying regulated yourself during challenging moments. Notice your own stress signals and use regulation techniques to maintain your calm. Your regulated presence is just as important as any specific strategy you implement.

Co-regulation works best when you have already built positive relationships with your students. Use the strategies you learned in Hack 4 to ensure you have developed that connection.

STEP 6: Nurture your own regulation practice.

Self-regulation is a key strategy because your emotional state directly impacts your students. When you can stay calm during challenging moments, you become a regulating presence that helps de-escalate rather than escalate situations.

Think about it: Students are constantly reading your energy. If you're stressed, anxious, or frustrated, they feel it immediately. Children's brains are wired to detect adult emotional states as a signal of safety or danger. A calm adult tells their internal systems that everything is okay. A dysregulated adult activates children's threat detection systems.

TAKING CARE OF YOURSELF IS ESSENTIAL, ESPECIALLY WHEN WORKING WITH STUDENTS AFFECTED BY TRAUMA.

Start with in-the-moment strategies. Notice your breathing when stress rises, and consciously slow it down. Take three deep breaths before responding to challenging behavior. Do a quick body scan to release tension in your shoulders, jaw, and hands. Lower your voice when chaos erupts.

Create longer-term practices, too. Find what helps you decompress after difficult days, whether that's a walk, music, talking with a friend, or sitting in silence for five minutes. Pay attention to your stress signals throughout the day so you can intervene before you reach your breaking point. Taking care of yourself is essential, especially when working with students affected by trauma.

OVERCOMING PUSHBACK

Regulation activities take away from instruction time. Dysregulated students are not fully benefiting from instruction anyway. Share with administrators how brief regulation activities improve focus and retention, more than making up for any lost instructional time. Document improvements in academic engagement when you provide students with regulation support. Point out that preventing dysregulation is far more efficient than managing crisis behaviors that can derail entire lessons. A two-minute breathing exercise that helps twenty-five students focus is more valuable than losing fifteen minutes to behavior management. Plus, nobody learns algebra while having a meltdown.

I don't have training in regulation techniques. You are off to a great start by reading this book! Begin with approaches like staying calm yourself and offering choices. Seek professional development opportunities, but remember that many effective co-regulation techniques, such as staying calm, speaking slowly, and offering comfort, are natural human responses that you already possess. Trust your instincts while you learn more formal strategies. Develop skills gradually, and have a few handy strategies that you are confident and comfortable using.

This work seems too focused on emotions rather than academics. Frame regulation support as brain science and learning readiness rather than emotional education. Help skeptical colleagues or families understand that regulation skills improve academic performance across all subjects. Share research about the connection between emotional regulation and cognitive function. Emphasize that you're not becoming a therapist; you're removing barriers to learning so students can access your academic content more effectively.

Some students don't participate in regulation activities. Offer choices and respect individual differences while modeling consistently. Some students need to observe before participating. Others may have cultural or personal reasons for preferring different approaches. The goal is to create opportunities, not to force participation. Make regulation activities optional but available, allowing students to engage at their comfort level. Sometimes, the most resistant students benefit from witnessing a classroom culture that values emotional wellness, even if they don't actively participate initially.

THE HACK IN ACTION

Ms. Hassan's junior English classes were filled with overwhelmed students dealing with college pressure, family expectations, and social stress. Rosa, who typically arrived argumentative and ready for conflict, would shut down completely during challenging discussions about literature.

Ms. Hassan began each class with a two-minute mindfulness moment—focused breathing, a brief reflection on the day ahead, or gentle movement to release tension. She also integrated stress management education into the study of literature, helping students analyze how characters managed adversity while teaching practical regulation skills.

Initially, students rolled their eyes and made jokes, but Ms. Hassan noticed changes within weeks. Rosa, who usually argued with peers within the first five minutes, was having fewer conflicts and began engaging more readily after the brief regulation time.

Ms. Hassan created a stress toolkit bulletin board with breathing techniques and local mental health resources. During a particularly challenging unit on trauma narratives, she provided trigger warnings and taught grounding techniques that students could use if the content became overwhelming.

By midyear, students were requesting longer mindfulness sessions before tests and asking to use regulation strategies during group-work conflicts. Rosa and several classmates privately shared that the techniques helped them manage stress at home and in other classes. Academic discussions became deeper as students felt safer taking intellectual risks.

Building regulation skills is a process, not a quick fix. Some students will need months or years to develop strong self-regulation, especially those who've experienced trauma or inconsistent caregiving. Your patient, steady support plants seeds that may not bloom until long after students leave your classroom.

The goal isn't perfect behavior or constant calm; it's helping students develop the skills they need to navigate big emotions, recover from difficult moments, and access their capacity for learning and growth. When we regulate before we educate, we're improving classroom management while teaching life skills that will serve students long after they've forgotten the academic content we taught.

REFLECTION
QUESTIONS

1. **How do you recognize when your students are dysregulated versus defiant?** Understanding the difference changes everything about your response. Dysregulation needs support and co-regulation, while true defiance might need clear boundaries and problem-solving.

2. **What regulation strategies work best for your specific students and grade level?** Individual differences matter enormously. Some students regulate through movement; others through quiet reflection. Some need more adult support; others prefer independence. Pay attention to what helps rather than what you think should help.

3. **How is your own regulation impacting your classroom environment?** Your emotional state is contagious. When you can stay calm during challenging moments, you become a regulating force for your students. When you're stressed and reactive, you can escalate situations unintentionally.

4. **Which students might benefit from individualized regulation plans?** While whole-class strategies help everyone, some students need additional support. Consider which children consistently struggle with regulation and how you might provide extra scaffolding for their success.

OFFER CHOICES TO BUILD AUTONOMOUS LEARNERS

Empower Students Within Appropriate Boundaries

Children learn how to make good decisions by making decisions, not by following directions.
— ALFIE KOHN, AUTHOR AND RESEARCHER

TWELVE-YEAR-OLD NOELLE SAT frozen at her desk, staring at the data analysis activity that had been placed in front of her. Around her, classmates were already writing, but her pencil remained motionless. She was in her third foster placement in eighteen months, and her fourth school. She'd learned that the safest strategy was to wait and watch. What were the rules here?

What happened if she got something wrong? What would trigger the adults in this room?

Mr. Nguyen noticed her hesitation and quietly approached. "Hey, Noelle, I see you're taking your time with this. That's totally fine. You have a few options for how you'd like to tackle this today. You could work on it solo, partner with someone, or we could go through the first few together. What sounds good to your brain right now?"

For the first time that day, Noelle looked up. Someone was asking what she wanted. Someone was giving her a say in her own learning. It was such a small moment, but for a student who had felt powerless for so long, it was everything.

"Could I ... could I try it by myself first and then ask for help if I need it?" she whispered.

"Absolutely. That sounds like a perfect plan."

What Mr. Nguyen understood, and what many educators are beginning to recognize, is that choice isn't a nice-to-have classroom management tool. For students who have experienced trauma, disruption, or powerlessness, meaningful choice becomes a pathway back to agency, confidence, and engagement. And here's the beautiful part: when we create classrooms that honor each student's need for autonomy, everyone benefits.

THE PROBLEM: WE'VE CREATED CHOICE-DEPRIVED CLASSROOMS

Walk into most classrooms and count how many decisions students make about their own learning. The number is shockingly small. Teachers decide what they'll learn, when they'll learn it, how they'll learn it, where they'll sit, who they'll work with, how they'll show what they know, and even when they can use the restroom. Then we wonder why some students push back, shut down, or seem disengaged.

For students who have experienced trauma, this lack of control can feel especially triggering. When children have lived through situations where they had no power over what happened to them, walking into a classroom where adults make every decision can activate their survival responses. They might become defiant, trying to hold onto whatever control they can grab. They might become compliant to the point of invisibility, afraid to make any choice at all. Or they might simply check out, protecting themselves by not caring about something they can't influence anyway.

> **WHEN YOU GIVE CHILDREN APPROPRIATE CHOICES WITHIN CLEAR BOUNDARIES, MAGIC HAPPENS. NOT CHAOS AND NOT ANARCHY. MAGIC.**

But it's not only our most vulnerable students who suffer from choice-deprived environments. All children have a fundamental need for autonomy. When we micromanage every aspect of their school experience, we're working against their natural development toward independence and critical thinking. We're teaching them to be passive recipients of education rather than active participants in their learning.

The result? Power struggles. Disengagement. Students who can perform well in school but can't think for themselves. And classrooms that feel more like compliance factories than communities of learners.

THE HACK: OFFER CHOICES TO BUILD AUTONOMOUS LEARNERS

Here's what we've learned from years of working with students who have experienced powerlessness: When you give children appropriate choices within clear boundaries, magic happens. Not chaos and not anarchy. Magic.

The Core Strategy: Offer Meaningful Choices Within Appropriate Boundaries

The crucial word here is "appropriate." We're not talking about letting students choose whether to learn math or follow safety rules. We're talking about meaningful choices within the structure you've established. Think of it like a restaurant menu. You still have to order food, but you get to choose what appeals to you from carefully curated options.

This approach recognizes that autonomy and structure aren't opposites, but allies. Students feel more empowered when they understand the boundaries within which they can make choices. Children who know they need to demonstrate their understanding of an area but can choose whether to do that through a game, a real-world application (such as designing a dream dorm room or planning a vegetable garden), or practice problems feel supported and empowered.

The core strategy is simple but transformative. Offer choices in how students learn, what they learn about, when they learn, where they learn, and how they show what they know. Start small, be consistent, and watch as your classroom transforms from a place where education happens to students to a place where students actively engage in their learning.

Offer Meaningful Choices

What makes a choice meaningful? First, you must be genuinely okay with any alternative you offer. Don't ask, "Do you want to go to lunch?" if lunch isn't negotiable. Don't offer three project choices if you secretly hope everyone picks the first one. Second, the choice should matter to the student in some way. Even small decisions like choosing between a red pen or a blue pen can help anxious students feel some control so they can get started. More substantial choices like whether to work quietly alone or talk through ideas with a partner give students agency over their learning experience.

For children exposed to trauma or instability, these choices become building blocks of trust and self-efficacy. Every time we honor their decision-making, we send the message, "Your thoughts matter. Your preferences are valid. You have power in this space." For students who've felt powerless, this affirmation can be revolutionary.

Offering choices doesn't mean lowering expectations or losing control of your classroom; the opposite tends to happen. When students feel they have genuine input into their learning experiences, they become more invested in the outcomes. They stop seeing their education as a requirement being done to them and start seeing it as a valuable effort they're actively creating.

Build Choice-Making Skills Gradually

Not all students come to us ready to handle complex decisions. Many have never been asked their opinion about learning, while others feel overwhelmed by too many options. The key is to scaffold choice-making skills like we scaffold academic learning.

Start with low-risk decisions with two or three options. For younger students, you might ask, "Would you like to sit on the carpet or at a table for story time?" For middle schoolers, ask, "Do you want to work on this individually or with a partner?" And for high schoolers, ask, "Would you prefer to write your reflection or record a video response?"

Pay attention to how students respond to choices. Some will immediately feel more engaged, while others might freeze up or always pick the same option. For students who struggle with decision-making, you can scaffold further by offering even smaller choices or thinking aloud about how you make decisions. "I'm choosing the blue marker because it shows up well on this paper" models decision-making processes.

Celebrate the choice-making process, not just the outcome. Commenting, "I noticed you really thought about that decision," or "You chose something that worked well for your learning style," helps students understand that good decision-making is a valuable skill.

As students become comfortable with basic choices, gradually increase the complexity. Move from choosing between two activities to choices with multiple options, such as deciding their research topic within the parameters you set. Eventually, some students will be ready to help design their learning goals and assessment methods.

Comfort with choice varies based on cultural background and individual experiences. Some students come from backgrounds where questioning authority or expressing preferences is discouraged. Others may have trauma histories that make any decision feel overwhelming. Be patient and meet students where they are, honoring their pace in developing autonomy.

WHAT **YOU** CAN DO TOMORROW

Ready to start giving your students more ownership over their learning experiences? You don't need to redesign your entire classroom overnight. Here are several ways to begin offering meaningful choices immediately.

- **Give students one learning position choice.**
  Tomorrow morning, tell your students, "Today you can choose to work at your desk, on the floor

with a clipboard, or standing at the tall table." That's it. Same assignment, same expectations, but suddenly, students have agency over their physical learning environment. You'll be amazed at how much more settled and focused they become when they can decide on the positions that work for their bodies and brains. For elementary students, you might add options like sitting on a cushion, using a stability ball, or working at a low table with its legs removed. Middle schoolers often love the option to stand or move to different areas of the room. High schoolers appreciate being trusted to find their optimal work environment, whether that's collaborating in the hallway or finding a quiet corner.

- **Offer topic choice within one assignment.** Instead of assigning "Write about your summer vacation," try "Write about a place that makes you feel happy. It could be your bedroom, somewhere you've traveled, or even somewhere you imagine." Same writing skills, same learning objectives, but now students get to draw from their experiences and interests. This adjustment is especially pow-erful for students whose summer experiences might not be the happy vacation memories we assume all kids have. The magic here is that you're still targeting the same learning goals, but you're allowing students to connect the assignment to their lives and interests. A student whose happy place is the local library, where they feel safe after school, has just as rich a story to tell as someone who went to Disney World or Europe.

- **Let students determine how they show their thinking.** "Show me your math work with numbers, pictures, or words—whatever makes sense to your brain." This phrase acknowledges that humans process and express ideas in different ways. Some kids are natural visual learners who think in pictures. Others need to talk through their reasoning. Still others prefer the precision of numerical work. This choice is particularly valuable for students who might have language barriers, learning differences, or cultural backgrounds that emphasize different ways of knowing. When we offer multiple ways to demonstrate understanding, we're not lowering the bar but removing barriers.

- **Create a choice board for one activity.** Grab a piece of paper and write three ways students can practice the same skill. For vocabulary development, it might be word sorts, creating sentences or stories using the words, or illustrating word meanings. For math concepts, choices could include hands-on games, real-world problem-solving, or explaining their thinking through drawings or words. It takes two minutes to create and gives students immediate ownership. The beauty of choice boards is that they can be as simple or elaborate as you want. Start with a handwritten list on chart paper. As you get more comfortable, you might create laminated boards with pictures or digital versions that students can access independently.

- **Ask one student to decide what would help them today.** Pick a student who's having a challenging moment and try saying, "I notice you're having a tough morning. What would help you feel successful right now?" Then really listen to the answer. Maybe the student needs to sit closer to you. Perhaps he needs a few minutes to collect himself. Maybe she needs a different way to approach the assignment. The key is that you're recognizing their expertise about their own needs and giving them agency in solving the problems. This approach is incredibly powerful for students who are used to adults making decisions about them rather than with them. It transforms you from someone who imposes solutions to someone who collaborates on them.

- **Use choice-based participation signals.** Here's a game-changer for classroom discussions: Try saying, "Raise your hand if you want me to call on you. Make eye contact or point to your brain if you're thinking. Put your thumb on your desk if you need more time." Suddenly, participation becomes collaborative rather than anxiety-provoking. Students who hate being randomly called on now feel safe. Students who love to share get their chance. Everyone's needs are honored. This is especially appreciated by children affected by trauma, whose responses might include shutting down when put on the spot unexpectedly.

A BLUEPRINT FOR FULL IMPLEMENTATION

Ready to go deeper? Creating a truly choice-rich classroom takes time and intentionality, but the transformation is worth every effort. Here's how to design a systematic approach to student autonomy.

STEP 1: Audit your current choice opportunities.

Spend a week paying attention to every decision you make for students. Carry a small notebook and jot down moments when you could ask, "What do you think?" or "How would you like to handle this?" You'll probably be surprised by how many opportunities exist.

Track academic choices (what, how, when, and where they learn), social choices (partners or groups), and environmental choices (seating, materials, and timing). Notice the patterns. Are there times of day when you're more controlling? Subject areas where you default to one-size-fits-all approaches? Students who rarely get asked for input?

This audit focuses on awareness. Most of us were educated in environments that lacked choice, so creating choice-rich classrooms requires conscious effort. The good news is that once you start noticing opportunities for choice, you'll see them everywhere.

STEP 2: Collect data to support your choice-rich classrooms.

Teachers may be concerned about how to track student progress when everyone is doing something different. The key is to focus on learning objectives and create systems that capture growth across multiple pathways.

Develop data collection methods that focus on standards mastery over assignment completion. Create basic tracking sheets that list learning objectives down one side and student names across the top, and indicate when students demonstrate mastery, regardless of which choice they used to get there. This data shows administrators that all students are meeting goals while honoring different learning paths.

Use digital tools to streamline choice-based data collection. Spreadsheets, Google Forms, and educational apps can help you track which students chose which options and how those choices affected their learning. Create drop-down menus with your common choice options so data entry becomes quick and consistent.

Build student self-assessment into your data collection system. When students reflect on their choices and learning, they provide valuable data about what's working. Paper or digital exit tickets, such as "Which choice helped you learn best today?" or "What would you choose differently next time?" provide insight into effectiveness while teaching students to evaluate their learning.

Create visual documentation that shows choice in action. Take photos of students working in their chosen formats, save examples of the ways students demonstrate the same concept, and keep brief notes about successful choice implementations. This evidence helps you communicate the value of choice-based learning to skeptical colleagues or administrators.

Design progress monitoring that works across different choice formats. Instead of comparing a poster to an essay, focus on whether both demonstrate an understanding of the same concepts. Create rubrics that can apply to multiple formats while maintaining consistent expectations for depth and quality of thinking.

STEP 3: Add choice into existing curriculum requirements.

Many teachers worry that they can't offer choices due to district mandates, pacing guides, or required textbooks. The solution isn't to abandon your requirements but to find creative ways to embed choice within existing structures.

Start with the learning objective, not the activity. If your curriculum requires students to understand cause and effect, they can explore it through historical events, science experiments, or literature analysis based on their interests. The standard stays the same while the pathway becomes flexible.

Create choice menus that align with required topics. If you must teach about the Revolutionary War, offer choices like creating a timeline, writing diary entries from different perspectives, or designing a museum exhibit. All options can address the same content standards while honoring different learning preferences.

Use required textbooks as one option among many. Instead of making everyone read Chapter 7, let students choose between the textbook, online articles, documentaries, or primary sources. They're still learning the required content, just through different entry points. An added bonus? Reading from multiple perspectives makes the classroom discussion much richer.

Include choice in required assessments by offering multiple formats that demonstrate the same skills. If your district requires persuasive writing, students might write traditional essays, craft a letter to the editor for the school newspaper, create infographics with persuasive text, outline key points to use in a debate, or develop presentation slides with strong arguments. The writing standards are met regardless of the format.

Work within pacing guides by offering choices about sequence and depth. Students might choose which unit to start with, which examples to explore deeply, or how much time to spend on different concepts, as long as everything gets covered by the deadline.

STEP 4: Troubleshoot common choice implementation challenges.

Even well-designed choice systems can lead to unexpected issues. Knowing how to address these common problems helps you preserve student independence while keeping learning on course.

When students always pick the same choice, it might signal comfort rather than laziness. Gently expand their options by pairing familiar choices with slightly new ones, or have conversations about trying different approaches. Sometimes, students need extra scaffolding to feel confident in branching out.

If choices create chaos or take too long, you've probably offered too many options too quickly. Scale back to two clear choices and gradually add complexity as students develop decision-making skills.

Address the "grass is greener" problem when students constantly want to switch choices mid-activity. Set clear expectations about commitment upfront and teach students to think through their decisions before making a selection. Help them understand that part of good decision-making is following through.

When some students seem overwhelmed by any choice, offer even smaller decisions or provide a default option they can fall back on. "Most people are choosing between A and B, but if you'd like me to choose for you today, I'll pick A." This message removes pressure while keeping the door open for future autonomy.

Handle complaints about unfairness when students see others doing different activities by teaching about various needs and learning styles. Use analogies like eyeglasses or Band-Aids. We don't all need the same supports, and that's okay. Help students understand that fair means everyone gets what they need, and they don't all need the same thing.

STEP 5: Build classroom systems for managing multiple pathways.

Once choice becomes central to your classroom, you need efficient systems to manage the variety without creating chaos for you or your students.

Design pick-and-choose panels and templates that you can reuse across different units. Create tracking systems so you know which students selected which options and how those choices worked out. The menu might be as simple as a paper chart on a clipboard or as sophisticated as a digital choice list that students can access independently. Digital options like Google Forms or Seesaw automatically track student choices in spreadsheets, while interactive Google Slides choice boards let students move their names to show their selections in real time.

Enhance the calming physical environment principles from Hack 5 by organizing your space to accommodate different learning preferences. Within your already regulation-supporting classroom, designate specific areas for quiet work, collaboration, and movement-friendly activities. Consider how students can access materials and resources independently when they are doing different activities simultaneously.

Develop assessment strategies that work across multiple pathways. Focus on the learning objectives that remain constant while allowing flexibility in how students demonstrate mastery. Create rubrics and scoring guides that you can apply to different types of products while maintaining consistent standards.

Build reflection routines into your choice-based activities. Help students think about how their choices affected their learning, what they might choose differently next time, and how they're growing as decision-makers. They can share these thoughts through surveys, journal entries, discussions, or thumbs-up, thumbs-down responses to your questions. This metacognitive work is just as valuable as the content learning.

Establish time management systems that prevent choice-making from becoming chaotic. Create clear signals for transition times, post estimated time requirements for different choices, and teach students to plan their workflow when they have options about sequence or pacing. Offer independent learning opportunities for students whose choices have them finishing before others.

STEP 6: **Foster student voice in classroom decisions.**

The goal is to move from teacher-directed choices to collaborative decision-making, where students have genuine input into how their classroom community functions.

Include students in the creation of classroom agreements. Ask for their input on seating arrangements, classroom jobs, celebration ideas, and problem-solving approaches. "Our current morning routine isn't working well. What ideas do you have?" This message shows students that their voices matter in shaping their environment.

Create consistent classroom meetings or community circles where students can raise concerns, suggest improvements, and celebrate successes together. These gatherings develop the relationships and communication skills that make shared decision-making possible.

TEACH THEM HOW TO COMMUNICATE THEIR PREFERENCES RESPECTFULLY, REQUEST ACCOMMODATIONS WHEN NEEDED, AND TAKE OWNERSHIP OF THEIR EDUCATIONAL EXPERIENCE.

At the elementary level, it might look like voting on class themes or choosing between activity options. Middle schoolers can provide input on assignment due dates, project formats, or classroom procedures. High schoolers might participate in curriculum planning, assessment design, or assisting with the interview process for new teachers.

Develop systems for collecting ongoing student feedback about choice implementation. Use surveys, exit tickets, or check-ins to understand what's working and what needs adjusting. Students often have the best insights about which choices feel meaningful and which ones feel like busywork.

Build students' capacity to advocate for their learning needs beyond your classroom. Teach them how to communicate their preferences respectfully, request accommodations when needed, and take ownership of their educational experience. These skills will serve them throughout their academic careers and beyond.

OVERCOMING PUSHBACK

When you shift from traditional, control-based teaching toward shared decision-making, you'll encounter some resistance. Here's how to address the most common concerns.

Too many choices are overwhelming for kids. This statement is true if you're not thoughtful about it. The solution isn't fewer choices—it's better choices. The key is to scaffold choice-making skills gradually, which we cover in detail at the beginning of this Hack and in Step 4. Start with two clear options and add complexity over time. Remember, feeling overwhelmed by choices is still better than feeling powerless.

Students make poor choices and then don't learn. This concern usually comes from a place of genuine care for student learning. The solution is to teach decision-making skills alongside offering choices and to build in natural consequences.

When a student chooses to work with friends but ends up socializing instead of learning, the natural consequence might be losing the choice to pick a partner next time. When someone chooses a project format they can't complete well, the learning happens in the reflection conversation afterward about what they'd do differently.

Recall that making poor choices and learning from them is part of a valuable education. We want students to practice decision-making in the safe environment of school when the stakes are lower than in the world outside the school walls.

I have to teach a specific, required curriculum and don't have flexibility. Choice doesn't mean abandoning your curriculum requirements. Start with the learning objective, not the activity. If students must understand fractions, they can explore them through cooking, sewing, or art projects based on their interests. Create an options list that aligns with the required standards—students might demonstrate their understanding of properties of matter by creating a Venn diagram, sorting attribute cards, or drafting a written explanation. Use required textbooks as one option among many, rather than the only source. Work within pacing guides by offering choices about sequence, depth, or examples while ensuring all content gets covered. You can find creative ways to embed choice within existing structures without reinventing your curriculum.

Offering choices takes too much planning time compared to having everyone do the same thing. The initial setup does require planning, but the systems you create (covered in Step 5) save time in the long term. Start with choices that need minimal preparation. Once you develop reusable templates and see how engaged students become, you'll find choice-based teaching more sustainable than traditional approaches.

THE HACK IN ACTION

Ms. Martinez had been teaching eleventh-grade American history for eight years when she decided to experiment with choice. Her students seemed increasingly disengaged, spending most of the class time on their phones or staring blankly at their textbooks. Behavior problems weren't dramatic, but the apathy was wearing her down. She started small, offering three options for demonstrating an understanding of the Progressive Era rather than requiring that everyone writes a five-paragraph essay.

The transformation was immediate. Students who had previously rushed through assignments spent extra time on projects they'd chosen. Quiet students found their voices through research formats that felt comfortable to them. Even her most challenging student, Sammy, who struggled with severe anxiety and initially begged her to "just tell me what to do," began investing in his work once he learned to navigate choices at his own pace.

But the real breakthrough came during a unit on social justice movements. Instead of assigning the same research paper to everyone, Ms. Martinez offered students the choice to become "experts" on different aspects of activism throughout American history. They could focus on labor rights, civil rights, women's suffrage, or environmental justice. They could present their learning through traditional research papers, documentary films, a podcast series, or by organizing a school awareness campaign.

What happened exceeded her wildest expectations. Students began collaborating naturally, seeking out classmates who were experts in areas that connected to their own research. They asked deeper questions because they were genuinely curious. They revised their work without being asked because they were proud of what they were creating.

Sammy, who typically froze when faced with decisions and had never shown an interest in history, initially felt overwhelmed by all the options. Ms. Martinez worked with him to narrow the possibilities, and he eventually chose to research the history of mental health awareness movements. Once he found a topic that connected to his own experiences in managing anxiety, his research became passionate and deeply personal. He interviewed school counselors, researched how societal understanding of mental health has evolved, and created a presentation that helped normalize conversations about anxiety among his peers. When he presented his findings about the stigma surrounding mental health throughout American history, you could hear a pin drop in the room.

"I never knew I could actually be good at research," he told Ms. Martinez afterward. "Having choices made it feel less scary somehow. Can I pick my topic next time, too?"

The shift wasn't just academic. The chronic low-level disruptions disappeared as students became invested in their learning community. Parent feedback was overwhelmingly positive, as well. Most importantly, Ms. Martinez rediscovered her love of teaching as she watched students become genuinely excited about learning.

By the end of the year, her students were self-directed learners who could formulate research questions, evaluate sources critically, and present compelling arguments. They had learned content, and they had learned how to learn.

When we offer students meaningful choices within appropriate boundaries, we're doing much more than improving engagement or reducing behavior problems. We're helping young people develop the confidence, critical thinking, and self-direction they'll need throughout their lives. We're showing them that their voices matter, their preferences are valid, and they have the power to shape their learning experiences.

For students who have felt powerless, this shift can be truly transformative. Plus, the benefits extend far beyond our most vulnerable learners. All students deserve to be active participants in their education. All students deserve to develop the decision-making skills they'll need as adults. All students deserve to experience the joy of learning when it connects to their interests, strengths, and goals.

Your classroom can be the place where students discover their agency. Offering them choices can help them develop the confidence to navigate an uncertain world. That's what life-changing education is all about.

REFLECTION QUESTIONS

1. **Where can you offer more meaningful choices in your current practice?** Look at your upcoming week and identify three specific moments when you could ask students for input instead of making decisions for them. Meaningful choices are ones where you can genuinely live with any option you offer.

2. **How do you balance structure with autonomy?** Consider the nonnegotiable boundaries in your classroom (safety, learning objectives, and respect for others) and the areas where flexibility is possible (methods, timing, topics, and social arrangements). The goal is to maximize student agency within clear expectations.

3. **What choices matter most to your students?** Different students value different types of autonomy. Some crave academic choices, others want social choices, and still others need environmental options. Pay attention to what energizes different learners, and offer variety that speaks to diverse needs.

4. **How can you help students who struggle with decision-making?** Some students, especially those who've experienced trauma or haven't had practice with choices, may need explicit support in developing decision-making skills. Consider how you can scaffold this learning while still honoring their growing autonomy.

5. **What messages are you sending about student capabilities?** Every choice you offer (or don't offer) communicates what you believe students can handle. Reflect on whether your practices match your stated beliefs about student potential and growth.

HACK 9

ASSIGN WITH EMPATHY

Reimagine Homework and Design a Trauma-Responsive Curriculum

When we know better, we do better.
— MAYA ANGELOU, AUTHOR AND POET

THE WORKSHEET SAT untouched in Malik's backpack for a week. When Ms. Kealani gently reminded him about it, he muttered, "I just didn't have time." She almost responded with a reminder about expectations, but then she remembered what she knew. Malik gets his little siblings off the bus every day. He makes dinner. He tucks them in. His evenings aren't free time; they're survival.

Across the room, Zayla stiffened when Ms. Kealani announced the Family Tree Research Project. While other students excitedly discussed which relatives they'd interview and which historical documents they'd explore, Zayla's eyes were fixed on her desk.

As a teen in her second foster placement this year, the assignment wasn't just difficult; it was impossible in its current form. Family histories, genealogy charts, and heritage presentations—these standard assignments become minefields for students navigating complex family situations.

Down the hall in Mr. Hayes's geometry class, Kelsi shifted uncomfortably as he explained the next project. "Map your bedroom to scale, including all furniture and measurements. This will help you understand spatial reasoning and real-world applications of coordinate geometry." The assignment seemed straightforward enough until you considered that Kelsi doesn't have a bedroom to map. She sleeps on her grandmother's couch, with her belongings stuffed into two garbage bags in the corner. Her classmate Eric was dealing with his own complications. He was staying at the emergency shelter this week, where room assignments changed nightly and personal space didn't exist.

In Ms. Moira's English class, the latest assignment was generating a quiet panic among students. "Research your family's immigration story and present it to the class. You'll need to interview relatives and find historical documents online." Kaden stared at the rubric, knowing he'd never be able to complete the research portion. His family didn't have internet access at home because the bill wasn't paid, and the public library closed before his shift at the grocery store ended. Even if he could access the internet, his grandmother, who raised him, barely spoke about the past; her memories were too painful to revisit.

Meanwhile, in the back of the room, Sofia pretended to take notes while inwardly cringing. Her assignment would involve fabricating an entire family narrative. As an undocumented student whose family had complex reasons for leaving their home country, the idea of researching and presenting their immigration story felt impossible and dangerous.

The chemistry teacher's latest project seemed innocent enough. "Create a family recipe and explain the chemical reactions involved in cooking. Include a video of you preparing the dish at home." For River, who'd been bouncing between relatives' houses and currently slept in his car, the assignment was a reminder of everything he didn't have—a kitchen, ingredients, and a stable home where filming wouldn't expose his living situation.

Mrs. Giordano once had a student refuse to participate in the Heritage Day celebration. After gentle questioning, she learned why. The student quipped, "Mrs. G, my mom's addicted to drugs, and my dad's in prison. That's my heritage. Want me to make a poster about that?"

Ouch.

These examples aren't isolated incidents. They're the daily reality in classrooms where well-meaning assignments accidentally exclude the very students who most need to feel included. Family trees, home drawings, parent interviews, and projects requiring stable internet access are assignments that become minefields for students navigating complex family situations, housing instability, or economic hardship.

THE PROBLEM: WE'RE DESIGNING ASSIGNMENTS FOR PRIVILEGE

Traditional school practices often operate under the assumption of stability, consistency, and conventional family structures. But for many students affected by trauma, these assumptions don't match their reality. When we design our curriculum and homework policies without considering diverse lived experiences, we unintentionally create barriers to learning and belonging, especially for the students who most need our support.

Remember the last time you tried to work in a noisy coffee shop? Or attempted to focus while your neighbor was doing construction?

Now imagine trying to complete homework in similar conditions every night. For many of our students affected by trauma, this is their reality.

For kids like Malik, homework isn't just another task; it's a nightly reminder of what they don't have: quiet space, adult support, stable routines, or even reliable electricity. Some students go home to take care of siblings, navigate housing insecurity, and manage adult-sized responsibilities. When we send work home without flexibility, we're essentially saying, "We know you're dealing with chaos, but could you please find a quiet corner in that chaos to diagram these sentences?"

> **TRADITIONAL ASSIGNMENTS OFTEN ASSUME A LEVEL OF STABILITY AND CONVENTIONAL FAMILY STRUCTURES THAT MANY OF OUR STUDENTS DON'T HAVE.**

And the problem is not just about homework. Our classroom assignments often come with invisible obstacles built right in. Like Kelsi trying to map a bedroom she doesn't have, or Sofia forced to choose between fabricating a family story or revealing dangerous truths about her immigration status. These scenarios play out in classrooms every day.

Many assignments overlook the fact that students come from vastly different home situations, where access to support, whether from caregivers or the environment, is not guaranteed. When we fail to consider these realities, we inadvertently create situations where some students must either expose painful truths, fabricate experiences, or disengage entirely. None of these options leads to learning.

Students like Zayla face particularly complex challenges. A family tree project becomes an exercise in explaining multiple placements, unknown biological history, or complicated legal situations. These students have often learned to protect their stories, yet our assignments sometimes force them to choose between sharing trauma or appearing non-compliant.

Even what we know about homework effectiveness is more complicated than most of us were taught. Education expert Alfie Kohn argues that homework provides minimal learning benefits while creating significant stress. Harris Cooper, whose research is often cited to support homework, found that homework has almost no benefit for elementary students and only moderate benefits for middle schoolers. What shows results? Targeted practice during the school day with teacher guidance and feedback.

For our students affected by trauma, the homework problem goes even deeper. Chronic stress affects executive functioning, including attention, organization, and time management. When students are in survival mode, their brains prioritize safety over schoolwork. It isn't defiance or laziness; it's their neurobiology saying, "Not now. I have bigger problems to solve."

We've created a system where assignments often reinforce privilege and penalize trauma. Students with stable homes, quiet study spaces, and supportive adults have built-in advantages, while those dealing with chaos, responsibility, or instability face additional barriers. When we don't account for these differences, we're not measuring learning; we're measuring circumstances.

THE HACK: ASSIGN WITH EMPATHY

So, what's the solution? Do we throw up our hands and say, "Well, some kids just can't do their homework"? Absolutely not. Instead, we reimagine both homework and classroom assignments with equity and trauma-responsiveness at the center. Think of it as creating a classroom where everyone can thrive, not only the students with Pinterest-perfect home lives.

Assigning with empathy doesn't mean eliminating expectations; it means designing them with humanity and inclusivity at the center. A trauma-responsive approach prompts us to reevaluate what we assign, why we assign it, and whether all students have a fair opportunity to succeed. When we shift from a compliance mindset to a care mindset, we can still hold high expectations, but we hold them alongside compassion.

The Core Strategy: Design Assignments and Curriculum That Remove Barriers While Maintaining High Expectations

This approach works because it acknowledges the reality that students come to us with vastly different resources, responsibilities, and experiences. Instead of pretending these differences don't exist, we design learning experiences that account for them. This work involves removing arbitrary barriers so that all students can reach the standards.

Reimagine Homework

First, let's tackle homework. Instead of assigning work that reinforces privilege and penalizes trauma, we can redesign it to honor students' lived realities.

What if we dedicated time during the school day for students to complete practice work? That twenty-minute block at the end of the day could be a game-changer for kids who don't have quiet homes. Some teachers call it Wrap-Up Time, others use Finish Strong, but the concept is the same: ensuring all students have access to the conditions they need for success.

What if we created flexible options that accommodate diverse home lives? Maybe Jayden can record his reading response instead of writing it. Perhaps Zoe could practice math facts during morning arrival instead of taking them home. The learning objective remains the same, but the pathway becomes accessible.

What if we removed grade penalties for incomplete homework,

especially when the reason stems from circumstances beyond students' control? A zero for not having a pencil at home seems like punishing poverty, not measuring learning. We can separate practice from assessment by using homework as formative feedback rather than evaluative judgment.

Transform Classroom Assignments

For classroom assignments, we can transform potentially triggering tasks into inclusive learning experiences.

Instead of traditional family trees, we might create Personal Influence Maps where students identify people, related or not, who have positively impacted their lives. This assignment celebrates meaningful connections without assuming everyone has a conventional family structure.

Instead of Draw Your Home projects, we could invite students to Design Your Dream Space, focusing on imagination and aspiration rather than on potentially complicated current realities. Rather than Mother's or Father's Day projects that assume traditional parental relationships, we might create Celebrating Special People activities that honor anyone significant in a student's life.

The shift is about removing arbitrary barriers so all students can meet the expectations. It's not "less than"; it's "different and maybe even better than."

WHAT YOU CAN DO TOMORROW

Ready to start creating more inclusive assignments without overhauling your entire curriculum? You can implement these shifts immediately to make a significant difference in ensuring all students can access and succeed with your learning objectives. Even small changes in how we design and present assignments can remove major barriers for our most vulnerable students.

- **Examine homework patterns in your classroom.** Who's completing assignments consistently? Who isn't? Look for patterns, especially along lines of socioeconomic status or family stability. Are your homework policies working for everyone, or just for students with stable support systems? This quick analysis will help you understand whether your current practices are equitable or are inadvertently penalizing students who lack home support.

- **Have honest conversations with students about their home realities.** Ask them about their routines, responsibilities, and challenges outside of school. You might discover that your "unmotivated" student is caring for an elderly grandfather every evening while both parents work the night shift. These conversations can be informal check-ins during independent work time or brief one-on-one chats as students are packing up. Listen without judgment and use this information to better understand the context behind incomplete assignments.

- **Create an end-of-day work block for assignment completion.** Even fifteen minutes can make a huge difference for students who don't have quiet study spaces at home. Call it Pack and Practice, Check and Reflect, or Homework Hurdle—whatever works for your classroom culture. Give students free time to catch up on assignments from your class or another class, ask questions while you're available to help, and ensure they have the supplies they need before heading home.

- **Implement a no-questions-asked homework pass system with clear boundaries.** Give students a few passes per quarter that they can use when life gets overwhelming. Create boundaries and limitations, such as stating that passes cannot be used for major projects or that only one can be used during a particular unit. This system isn't a get-out-of-learning-free card; it's a way for students to advocate for their needs without shame while maintaining academic expectations and responsibility.

- **Do a trauma scan of your next assignment.** Are you asking students to share information about their families, homes, or personal histories that might be painful for some? Does this assignment assume students have baby photos, stable housing, or traditional family structures? If so, create options that allow students to engage with the same learning objectives without requiring personal disclosure. For example, instead of "family tree," try "people who influence me," or instead of "describe your bedroom," offer "explain your ideal learning space."

- **Adjust your language to be more inclusive.** Instead of "Ask your parents to sign this," try "Ask your grown-up or adult to sign this." Instead of

FROM BREAKDOWNS TO BREAKTHROUGHS

"Draw your family," try "Draw people who are important to you." These subtle shifts signal that you recognize and honor family diversity while making assignments accessible to students in foster care, kinship care, or non-traditional family structures.

A BLUEPRINT FOR FULL IMPLEMENTATION

Ready to systematically transform your assignment practices? Building a truly trauma-responsive approach to homework and classroom projects requires intentional planning and gradual implementation. This work ensures that every student has an equitable opportunity to demonstrate their learning. Here's your roadmap for creating assignments that work for all students.

STEP 1: Establish Universal Design for Learning (UDL) principles.

Creating a classroom that works for all students from the start requires systematic planning across three UDL domains: choice, representation, and expression. For engagement, offer choice in topics whenever possible. If students must demonstrate their understanding of fractions, let the animal enthusiast use pet examples while the chef-in-training adjusts recipes by halving ingredients. Create assignment menus that honor different interests and cultural backgrounds while meeting the same learning objectives.

For representation, provide multiple ways for students to access information. Some students need visual supports, others benefit from audio processing, and many require hands-on manipulation.

Design lessons where the same concept is presented through stories, diagrams, physical models, and real-world applications.

For expression, revolutionize how students demonstrate learning. Traditional written reports become choice menus: create a documentary, design an infographic, build a model, record a podcast, or write a traditional essay. Each option requires the same depth of understanding but allows students to showcase their learning by using their strengths.

Grade-level considerations matter. Elementary students might choose between drawing, acting out, or dictating their responses. Middle schoolers could select from individual projects, collaborative presentations, or community action plans. High schoolers might opt for research papers, artistic interpretations, or internship connections.

Create template systems that make this sustainable. Develop option charts for frequently taught concepts, establish classroom norms around choice-making, and build student decision-making skills explicitly. When students understand that different pathways lead to the same rigorous learning, they stop seeing accommodations as special treatment and start viewing them as smart learning strategies.

STEP 2: Develop a trauma-sensitivity checklist for all assignments.

Before implementing any assignment, systematically evaluate it through a trauma-responsive lens using these essential questions: Does this require sharing personal or family information that students might want to keep private? Does this assume access to resources (internet, quiet space, or adult support) that some students lack? Could this trigger difficult memories for students with complex backgrounds? Are we inadvertently creating situations where students must choose between honesty and safety?

Develop red-flag awareness for problematic language. Assignments asking students to "share a happy family memory" or "write about your favorite vacation" might seem innocent, but they can be landmines for students in foster care, experiencing homelessness, or dealing with family trauma. Similarly, phrases like "ask your parents" exclude students living with grandparents, with guardians, or in kinship care. Change your vocabulary to "ask your adult."

Create green-light alternatives that maintain learning objectives while removing barriers. Instead of "family tree," try "my personal role models." Rather than "describe your home," offer "describe a dream studio, lab, or workshop where you could explore your passions." Replace "interview a parent about their childhood" with "interview any adult about their experiences."

Add assignment flexibility into your planning process. For every assignment, identify the core learning objective and brainstorm at least three ways students could demonstrate that learning. Document what works through tracking systems; note which students choose which options and how successfully they meet learning goals. These observations can help you individualize future assignments around your students' interests and needs.

Establish review partnerships with colleagues who can offer fresh perspectives on potential triggers you might miss. Sometimes, we're too close to our curriculum to see embedded assumptions or biases. Having a fresh set of eyes can help you see things that you might have missed or not even considered. We all have diverse experiences. What might be neutral to one person could evoke a strong emotional reaction in another. Your review partners can identify areas that might unintentionally cause emotional distress. Assignment audits should become as routine as checking for typos. Inviting trusted educators to provide feedback and suggestions can help us create more inclusive learning experiences.

STEP 3: **Restructure homework practices systematically.**

Begin by honestly examining your current homework effectiveness. Track completion rates, quality of work, and the correlation with actual learning. Many teachers discover that homework creates stress without improving outcomes, particularly for students facing home challenges.

Transition gradually to minimize pushback. Start by reducing the amount of homework while increasing in-school practice time. Create a list of homework options that fit their home circumstances. Reading to a sibling counts as literacy practice, helping with grocery shopping becomes real-world math, and family conversations about current events substitute for traditional research assignments.

Redesign your daily schedule to include substantial student work time, which might mean longer class periods with built-in practice time, study halls that focus on studying, or arrival/departure times used for assignment completion. Ensure that students have access to the necessary materials (pencils, calculators, and internet access) during school hours rather than assuming home availability. If at-home work is necessary, create homework bags that include sharpened pencils, scissors, and other supplies for students who might need them.

Completely separate practice from assessment. Homework becomes formative feedback for you and students to understand learning progress, not evaluative data that impacts grades. Students who can't complete home practice aren't penalized; instead, they receive additional support during school time. If students can demonstrate their understanding of a concept or skill at school, why do they need to repeat it at home? And if they are struggling to grasp it in class, what makes us think that more of the same practice problems to do at home will change that?

Develop communication strategies for families who expect traditional homework. Emphasize that your new approach prioritizes learning effectiveness over homework compliance. For younger students, describe how research shows that minimal academic benefit is obtained from traditional homework, while for older students, quality and meaningful practice matter more than quantity. Highlight how school-based practice allows for immediate teacher feedback and support across grade levels. Share data showing improved learning outcomes when students aren't battling homework stress. Many families will thank you for removing the added burden from their daily routine while ensuring their children still receive rigorous academic preparation.

Create systems for students who need additional practice. Some students thrive on extra challenges or genuinely prefer working at home. Offer optional extension activities, independent projects, or advanced practice for students who request it, while ensuring that these add-ons aren't requirements in disguise.

STEP 4: Create a culture of inclusive accommodations.

Transform accommodations from special exceptions into the usual classroom practice. When you announce assignment choices, use language like, "Everyone's brain works differently, so we have multiple ways to show your amazing thinking today!" This process normalizes options while celebrating neurodiversity.

Teach students about learning differences explicitly. Share how different professionals use various tools. Architects use visual thinking, musicians use auditory processing, and athletes use kinesthetic intelligence. Help students understand that accommodations aren't crutches; they're tools that help people access their capabilities.

Establish choice-making protocols that prevent overwhelm. Rather than offering unlimited options, provide two to three clearly defined choices that meet the same learning objective. Create a homework grid that helps students select appropriate options quickly. Teach decision-making skills explicitly because some students have never been offered educational choices and need support to advocate for their needs.

Ensure that all options can be assessed fairly by creating clear rubrics that focus on the learning objective rather than the format. For older students, involve them in defining assessment categories on the rubric, as their involvement increases ownership and helps them understand how different approaches to the same assignment will be evaluated.

Encourage peer understanding through community discussions. When students ask, "Why does she get to do something different?" respond with teaching moments about fairness versus equality. Use analogies like eyeglasses. We don't think it's unfair that some people wear glasses to see clearly, and we shouldn't think it's unfair that some people need different tools to learn effectively.

Document what works for individual students without creating a stigma. Tracking systems help you remember which approaches support each learner best. This information becomes invaluable for advocacy during team meetings and transitions to new teachers. Frame documentation as learning profiles rather than accommodation lists to maintain strengths-based perspectives.

STEP 5: Examine practices through a trauma-responsive lens.

Establish routine review cycles for all assignments and policies. Monthly team meetings should include agenda items for examining recent assignments through equity and trauma-sensitivity lenses. Quarterly curriculum reviews should specifically address whether current practices create barriers for vulnerable students.

Develop data collection systems that go beyond traditional metrics. Track completion rates and test scores, but also student engagement, stress levels, and feedback about assignment accessibility. Exit tickets asking, "Did you feel successful with today's assignment?" can provide valuable insights into student experiences.

Create student feedback mechanisms that honor their expertise about their learning needs. Regular surveys, suggestion boxes, or focus groups help you understand which practices support or hinder different learners. Students often have insights about assignment barriers that adults miss entirely.

Design collaboration systems with colleagues who serve diverse populations. Special education teachers, English learner specialists, counselors, and social workers bring crucial perspectives about potential assignment challenges. Their input during planning stages can prevent problems, saving the time it takes to fix them.

Establish professional development priorities around trauma-responsive teaching. Attend workshops, read current research, and engage in collaborative learning about best practices. This work requires ongoing growth and reflection, not a one-time training. Connect with educators doing similar work to share strategies and learn from each other's successes and challenges.

STEP 6: Build systems for ongoing support.

Create sustainable support systems that extend beyond individual teachers to encompass whole-school transformation. This process requires building capacity at multiple levels and ensuring trauma-responsive assignment practices become institutional rather than dependent on individual educator commitment.

Develop student self-advocacy skills explicitly. Teach students to recognize their learning needs, communicate effectively about challenges, and request appropriate support. Create scripts and role-play scenarios that help students practice asking for help without shame. Many children affected by trauma have learned to hide struggles, so explicit instruction in advocacy becomes a crucial life skill development.

Train paraprofessionals, volunteers, and support staff in trauma-responsive approaches. These team members often provide critical assignment support but lack training in recognizing trauma responses or implementing inclusive practices. Brief training modules help ensure consistent, supportive approaches across all student interactions.

Develop administrative understanding and policy support. Share data about positive outcomes from trauma-responsive assignment practices with principals and district leaders. Advocate for policy changes that support flexibility, such as grading practices that separate learning from compliance, homework policies that honor family diversity, and assessment approaches that offer multiple demonstration methods.

Connect with community resources that support student success. Partner with local libraries that offer quiet study spaces, community centers with after-school programs, or organizations serving specific populations like youth in the foster care system or refugee families. These partnerships extend support beyond school hours while honoring the reality that not all students have ideal home learning conditions.

Establish mentorship and coaching systems for educators implementing these practices. Change is challenging, and sustained implementation requires ongoing support. Peer coaching, observation partnerships, and regular reflection opportunities help teachers refine their practice while building the school-wide capacity for trauma-responsive education. This system creates sustainable transformation rather than isolated individual efforts.

OVERCOMING PUSHBACK

When you start redesigning assignments with trauma sensitivity in mind, you'll likely face questions from colleagues, administrators, and parents who worry about lowering standards or enabling students. These concerns come from a place of caring, but they're often based on misconceptions about what equitable teaching looks like. Here's how to address the most common concerns while staying committed to inclusive practices.

Students will take advantage of the situation. Will some students try to game the system? Perhaps. But in our experience, most don't. And those who do are usually signaling a need, not a character flaw. We'd rather have a few students occasionally take advantage than have many students regularly feel defeated. Trust is the foundation of trauma-responsive practice. If a student consistently avoids assignments, they're communicating that something isn't working.

Parents expect traditional assignments. True, but expectations can evolve when we communicate thoughtfully. Frame these changes as elevating rigor and learning, not diminishing them. Share the research showing that inclusive assignments often produce higher-quality work because students can focus on content rather than navigating triggers. Send home simple explanations that emphasize your commitment to helping all students achieve their potential.

But these are our school traditions! Yes, and traditions can evolve. When we know better, we do better. The Family Heritage project can become a Cultural Influences project. The Mother's Day craft can become a Special Person gift. The core intention remains, but the execution becomes inclusive rather than exclusive.

Students need to learn to deal with difficult emotions. That statement is true. But there's a difference between productive challenge and unnecessary trauma activation. Students can't learn when they're in survival mode. Creating a safe environment allows students to practice managing their emotions productively rather than being blindsided by assignments that trigger trauma responses without support.

The real world won't accommodate them. Actually, the real world offers far more flexibility than most schools. In workplaces, adults have choices about when, where, and how they complete tasks. When we teach students to identify barriers and find alternative pathways to success, we're giving them the skills they'll need in work, relationships, and lifelong learning.

THE HACK IN ACTION

Let's see what trauma-responsive assignment practices look like in real classrooms across different grade levels.

Ms. Abney, a fifth-grade teacher in a Title I school, noticed a troubling pattern. Students who participated eagerly in class were accumulating zeros in the gradebook for homework they couldn't complete. She'd tried planners, reminders, and parent calls. Nothing changed the fundamental problem: many of her students simply didn't have the home conditions necessary for traditional homework completion.

So she tried a revolutionary tactic. She eliminated traditional homework and built a twenty-minute block into the end of each day called Wrap-Up Time. Students used it to read, work on assignments, or get help. Those who needed more time were offered homework passes with no penalty or explanation required.

The change was remarkable. The anxiety around homework disappeared. Students stayed engaged, families reported fewer tears at home, and Ms. Abney saw her classroom culture shift: students felt seen, respected, and capable. She hadn't lowered expectations; she'd raised equity.

* ❀ *

In middle school, Mr. Rivera had always assigned a family history project as part of his immigration unit. Students would interview family members about their origins and create presentations. It was a beloved school tradition that seemed to engage students and families.

After learning about trauma-responsive teaching, he realized that this assignment created unseen barriers for many students, particularly those in foster care, those with family estrangement, or those whose family histories included forced migration or other traumas. He redesigned the project as Journeys That Matter, allowing students to explore any significant journey, whether physical, cultural, or personal.

Students could research historical migrations, interview community members, or explore their own experiences if they chose. The project still achieved its learning goals while becoming accessible to all.

The results were transformative. Students who had previously disengaged produced thoughtful, passionate work. One student in the foster care system, who had been silent during previous family projects, created a powerful presentation about a refugee community in their city. Another, whose parent was incarcerated, explored the journey of a favorite athlete who had overcome obstacles.

Mr. Rivera discovered that by removing the assumption of a traditional, knowable family history, he'd created space for deeper, more authentic learning for everyone.

When we design assignments with empathy, we shift from a system that rewards privilege to one that nurtures potential. We used to think fairness meant treating everyone the same. Now we understand that true equity means giving each student what they need to succeed. Sometimes, that means offering alternatives. Sometimes, it means adding in support. And every time, it means seeing our students as whole humans with complex lives beyond our classroom walls.

The most powerful learning happens when students feel safe, seen, and capable. By reimagining our approaches to homework and classroom assignments, we create that essential foundation, especially for students whose lives outside of school may be chaotic or challenging. When we focus on connection over compliance, we discover that high expectations and deep compassion aren't opposing forces; they're partners in creating classrooms where every student can thrive.

REFLECTION
QUESTIONS

1. **Which of your current assignments might create unintended barriers for students with trauma histories or non-traditional family structures?** Consider obvious triggers and subtle assumptions embedded in your practices.

2. **How could you redesign your homework policy to support equity while maintaining high learning expectations?** Think about alternatives that honor diverse home circumstances while still promoting practice and growth.

3. **What assumptions about students' home lives or family structures might be embedded in your curriculum?** Look beyond the obvious family tree assignments to more subtle expectations about resources, support, and stability.

4. **If you were to implement one change tomorrow to make your assignments more inclusive, what would it be?** Start small, but start somewhere, recognizing that even minor shifts can have major impacts on vulnerable students.

HACK 10

COLLABORATE FOR WHOLE-SCHOOL CHANGE

Establish Support Networks for Students and Educators

*Never doubt that a small group of thoughtful,
committed citizens can change the world;
indeed, it's the only thing that ever has.*
— MARGARET MEAD, ANTHROPOLOGIST

Mrs. Washington had been implementing trauma-responsive practices in her fourth-grade classroom for two years, and the transformation was undeniable. Her students were more engaged, behavioral incidents had dropped dramatically, and families were commenting on the positive changes they saw at home. But Mrs. Washington felt like she was running a marathon while everyone else was walking in the opposite direction.

Every day, her students left her nurturing classroom environment and encountered jarring inconsistencies throughout the school. In the cafeteria, adults yelled at children who were too noisy. The music teacher still used a public behavior chart that humiliated struggling students. The principal's office had become either a place of punishment or, worse, an unintentional reward center where struggling students got to color, play with Legos, or relax while avoiding the academic demands they found overwhelming. When students discovered that throwing a chair in the art teacher's class led to a peaceful morning of drawing in the office, the cycle perpetuated itself. Mrs. Washington watched her students, who had learned to trust and regulate in her space, become dysregulated again as they navigated conflicting expectations and approaches.

Meanwhile, down the hall, new teacher Mr. Morales was drowning. He'd attended one workshop on trauma-responsive teaching and desperately wanted to make changes, but he felt overwhelmed and unsure about where to start. He'd tried implementing a few strategies from that single training, but without ongoing support, coaching, or colleagues to brainstorm with, he quickly reverted to the behavior management techniques he'd learned in student teaching when faced with challenging situations.

Across the building, veteran educator Ms. O'Brien was skeptical of what she saw as the latest educational fad. She'd survived countless initiatives that promised to revolutionize teaching, from brain-based learning to backward design to whatever education acronym was trending on social media that month. "Trauma-informed, trauma-responsive"—it all sounded like more buzzwords that would add more work to her already overwhelmed plate. She needed to see concrete evidence that these approaches worked before she'd invest her limited time and energy.

In the front office, the principal, Ms. Adebayo, genuinely cared about her students but struggled to understand why some teachers seemed to coddle kids while others maintained firm boundaries. She wanted consistency across her building but wasn't sure how to achieve it when her staff seemed to have such different philosophies about student behavior and expectations.

These scenarios play out in schools across the country. Teachers burn out from swimming against the current, administrators feel caught between competing approaches, and students don't receive the consistent, healing support they desperately need.

THE PROBLEM: WE'RE WORKING IN ISOLATION WHEN WE NEED COMMUNITY

Here's what no one wants to admit about trauma-responsive education. It is difficult for teachers to sustain when working in isolation. When implementation varies wildly across a school, even the most dedicated individual efforts get undermined by systemic inconsistency.

Students who have experienced trauma need predictability to feel safe enough to learn. When they encounter dramatically different behavioral expectations, communication styles, and adult responses as they move between classrooms, the cafeteria, specials, and the main office, they stay in survival mode—anxious, confused, and often disruptive. A child who finally learns to trust and regulate in one supportive classroom may fall apart all over again when faced with harsh or punitive approaches elsewhere in the building. When practices are inconsistent, it adds to the hyper-alertness that trauma creates, making it nearly impossible for students to feel safe to learn and grow.

Individual teachers attempting trauma-responsive practices without support are more likely to face burnout and frustration. They pour tremendous energy into creating healing environments, only to watch their students struggle in other spaces. They may feel criticized by colleagues who view their approaches as too lenient or questioned by administrators who don't understand why they're not using traditional disciplinary measures. Without professional development, coaching, and collaborative problem-solving opportunities, even the most committed educators eventually feel isolated and exhausted.

Inconsistencies in expectations are challenging for all students. But children who have been in the foster care system and other students with complex trauma histories get hit with a double whammy. They're already dealing with all the neurobiological impacts of trauma, and then they're thrust into school environments where adults respond to their needs in totally different (and often contradictory) ways. One teacher offers comfort and understanding while another demands compliance and control. The computer teacher uses public shaming tactics while the paraprofessional builds private relationships. This inconsistency can *retraumatize* students who are working hard to trust the adults in their school community.

Perhaps most concerning is how these isolated efforts create stigma rather than understanding. When only one or two teachers in a building implement trauma-responsive approaches, students who need those supports can become labeled as "Mrs. Smith's kids" or "the trauma kids." This labeling creates shame for students and resistance from other educators who may feel their methods are being criticized.

Even when teachers have figured out effective strategies, schools too often miss opportunities for collaborative problem-solving and shared expertise. Teachers aren't given in-school time to share insights and strategies with their colleagues. Specialists like counselors, social workers, and special education teachers aren't included in conversations about classroom-based trauma supports. Administrators create policies without understanding how those decisions might impact students affected by trauma.

The result is educational environments that are inconsistent, inequitable, and ineffective for the students who need the most support. We end up with pockets of excellence surrounded by confusion rather than comprehensive cultures of care.

THE HACK: COLLABORATE FOR WHOLE-SCHOOL CHANGE

Creating lasting change requires moving from individual implementation to collective transformation. The most effective trauma-responsive schools don't just happen—they're intentionally built through collaboration, shared professional learning, and systematic policy alignment.

Rather than mandating that every teacher implements identical practices or forcing reluctant staff to embrace new approaches overnight, aim to create a culture where trauma-responsive practices become the natural way we work with students because the methods make sense, they work, and they're supported at every level.

The Core Strategy: Build Collaborative Teams That Function

Effective school-wide change starts with identifying and connecting educators who are already interested in trauma-responsive approaches. You don't need everyone on board from day one—you need a critical mass of willing participants who can model effective practices and gradually influence others through their results.

Start by finding your allies. Look for colleagues who already demonstrate empathy with students, who ask questions about the underlying causes of behavior, or who express frustration with punitive approaches that don't seem to work. These educators become your initial collaborative team, regardless of their formal roles or grade levels.

Create periodic, structured opportunities for this team to meet, share strategies, and problem-solve together. It might be a monthly lunch meeting, a standing professional learning community, or an informal after-school gathering. Consistency and genuine collaboration are more effective than top-down professional development.

Focus early meetings on sharing successes and challenges rather than trying to learn new techniques. When teachers see concrete examples of how trauma-responsive practices work in real classrooms with real students, they become much more willing to try new approaches themselves.

Gradually expand your collaborative network by inviting interested colleagues to join your conversations. Word spreads quickly when teachers discover a supportive group where they can openly discuss student challenges without judgment and share practical strategies.

Develop a Shared Understanding Through Professional Learning

One-shot workshops on trauma-responsive teaching rarely create lasting change because they don't provide ongoing support or address the complex challenges teachers face when implementing new approaches. Effective professional learning happens over time through multiple formats and focuses on practical application in addition to the theoretical concepts.

Design professional learning experiences that meet teachers where they are, and avoid overwhelming them with information they can't use immediately. Start with the basic concepts about how trauma affects learning and behavior, then gradually add more specific strategies for classroom implementation.

Use real student scenarios from your classroom or school to make the learning relevant and immediate. When teachers can see how trauma-responsive approaches might help the actual students they teach, they're much more likely to try new strategies. Anonymize examples appropriately, but make them specific enough to be meaningful.

Provide multiple ways for teachers to engage with trauma-responsive concepts. Some educators learn best through reading and research, others through hands-on practice, and still others through collaborative discussion. Offer book studies, strategy-sharing sessions, classroom observations, and informal mentoring relationships.

DISCIPLINE THAT DOESN'T CONSIDER UNDERLYING CAUSES, HOMEWORK POLICIES THAT ASSUME STABLE HOME ENVIRONMENTS, AND ATTENDANCE PROCEDURES THAT DON'T ACCOUNT FOR COURT DATES AND PLACEMENT CHANGES ALL PUNISH STUDENTS FOR CIRCUMSTANCES BEYOND THEIR CONTROL.

Add in time for teachers to reflect on their experiences and triggers. Adults who have experienced trauma may find this work personally challenging, and educators who haven't may struggle to understand their students' responses. Create safe spaces for processing these reactions without requiring anyone to share personal information.

Connect your trauma-responsive professional learning to existing school initiatives. Show how these approaches support, not compete with, your literacy goals, behavior expectations, and academic standards.

Create Systematic Policy Alignment

The most well-intentioned trauma-responsive practices will fail if they conflict with existing school policies around discipline, attendance, grading, and family engagement. Lasting change requires examining these policies through a trauma-responsive lens and making necessary adjustments.

Start by conducting a policy audit with your collaborative team. Review your school's discipline procedures, homework expectations, attendance policies, and parent communication practices. Ask hard questions about how these policies might impact students who have experienced trauma, particularly those in foster care or other unstable living situations.

Look for policies that inadvertently penalize students for trauma responses. Zero-tolerance discipline that doesn't consider underlying causes, homework policies that assume stable home environments, and attendance procedures that don't account for court dates and placement changes all punish students for circumstances beyond their control. These policies need immediate examination and revision.

Advocate for policy changes that support trauma-responsive practices while maintaining high expectations for all students. Policy changes might involve creating alternatives to suspension, developing flexible homework options, or establishing restorative practices for addressing conflicts.

Work with administrators to align building-wide expectations with trauma-responsive principles. If your school motto states that it values respect, safety, and learning, help leadership see how trauma-responsive approaches strengthen these values.

Document the positive outcomes of policy changes to gather support for further modifications. When you can show that trauma-responsive policies reduce office referrals, improve attendance, or increase academic engagement, skeptical colleagues and administrators become more willing to consider additional changes.

Support Adult Well-Being

Teachers can't pour from empty cups, and implementing trauma-responsive practices can be emotionally demanding work. Schools serious about whole-system change must address the well-being of adults alongside the needs of students.

Acknowledge that working with children affected by trauma creates secondary trauma for educators. Provide resources and support for teachers who may be experiencing emotional responses to student stories and behaviors. This support might include access to counseling services, stress management workshops, or permission to take breaks when needed.

Cultivate a school climate where asking for help is seen as a professional strength rather than a personal weakness. Teachers need to feel safe admitting when they're struggling with particular students or situations without the fear of being labeled ineffective.

Create regular opportunities for debriefing and processing challenging situations with colleagues. Sometimes, teachers need to talk through what happened, get reassurance that they handled situations appropriately, or brainstorm different approaches for next time.

Celebrate the small victories and progress that might not show up on standardized tests but represent meaningful growth for students affected by trauma. Recognition and validation help sustain teachers through the challenging aspects of this work.

Address workload concerns honestly and realistically. If trauma-responsive practices initially require additional time and energy, help teachers identify other tasks they can streamline or eliminate to make space for this essential work.

WHAT **YOU** CAN DO TOMORROW

You can implement these five actions immediately, without permission from administration or a commitment from reluctant colleagues. Starting small creates the momentum for larger changes while providing immediate support for students.

- **Identify one colleague to connect with about trauma-responsive practices.** Look for someone who is compassionate toward their students and approaches their behaviors with curiosity instead of judgment. It might be a grade-level partner, a special education teacher, a counselor, or anyone else who seems genuinely interested in understanding student behavior. These are the people who are likely practicing trauma-responsive care, whether or not they call it that.

- **Review one school policy through a trauma-responsive lens.** Select one school-wide policy or procedure and ask yourself how it might impact a student in foster care, a child whose parent is deployed, or a family experiencing housing instability. Look for unintended barriers or consequences that might penalize or retraumatize vulnerable students.

- **Share one specific strategy that's working in your classroom.** Mention a trauma-responsive approach you've tried and the positive results you've seen, whether you talk about it in a casual hallway conversation, a team meeting, or an email to a colleague. Be specific about what you did and how students responded. This plants the seeds for others to try similar approaches.

- **Document inconsistencies you notice across your school.** Keep notes about different expectations students encounter in various settings— cafeteria rules versus classroom expectations, office procedures versus specials classes, and playground supervision styles versus indoor interactions. This documentation isn't to call out your colleagues; it's a valuable tool when advocating for school-wide alignment.

- **Address one instance of stigma or bias you observe.** When you hear a colleague make deficit-based comments about a student's behavior, family situation, or background, gently offer a reframe. Instead of staying silent when someone says a child is manipulative, you might respond with, "I wonder if they're trying to feel safe," or "That sounds like a trauma response to me." Often, these comments come from misinformation or a perspective that has not been considered. Plus, every time you speak up, you help shape the culture where compassion and understanding are the norm.

A BLUEPRINT FOR FULL IMPLEMENTATION

Moving from individual efforts to comprehensive school transformation requires systematic planning and sustained commitment. This blueprint provides a roadmap for creating lasting change while acknowledging that implementation timelines will vary based on school context and readiness.

STEP 1: Build awareness and launch the initiative.

Start small with two or three willing colleagues who already show interest in supporting students who struggle. You don't need to convince everyone at once. Share brief success stories and data points about trauma-responsive approaches when natural opportunities arise in team meetings or casual conversations.

> STARTING SMALL CREATES THE MOMENTUM FOR LARGER CHANGES WHILE PROVIDING IMMEDIATE SUPPORT FOR STUDENTS.

If you have administrative support, work together to present evidence to the rest of the staff. If not, focus on building grassroots interest one conversation at a time. This awareness phase might take several months, and that's perfectly normal.

Form a small collaborative team once you find a few interested people. Meet monthly over lunch or after school, keeping it informal and sustainable. Your goal is for mutual support and strategy sharing.

Resistance is normal and doesn't reflect the value of this work. Focus on the educators who are ready to learn rather than trying to convert skeptics. If you've tried to implement a change in a school, you know that it's not easy to get educators to agree.

Often, seeing positive results in action becomes the most powerful awareness-building tool.

STEP 2: Gather data and evidence.

Work with your administrators to access existing school data, such as office referrals and suspension patterns. If this isn't possible, start documenting what you observe in your classroom and grade level.

Ask your team members to notice inconsistencies they encounter as they move through the building, and keep notes about what students experience differently across settings. This informal observation can be as valuable as formal surveys.

Connect with colleagues who are already implementing trauma-responsive practices successfully. Learn from their experiences rather than starting from scratch.

Don't feel pressure to conduct formal research or comprehensive data collection. Sometimes, the most compelling evidence comes from tracking one student's progress over time or documenting how a single strategy change affected your classroom climate. Small-scale documentation can be as powerful as district-wide statistics.

STEP 3: Craft your approach.

Advocate for professional development opportunities rather than trying to train everyone yourself. Share resources like book titles (hint, hint), workshop information, or experts in your area with administrators who make professional development decisions.

Within your team, identify one or two specific policy areas that need the most attention, and focus your energy. Present specific suggestions, not general complaints, to the administration.

Plan how your small team will take what you're learning and share it with interested colleagues, such as through informal hallway conversations, in brief team meeting shares, or by offering to mentor new teachers.

Create a timeline that spans one to two years, not months. Sustainable change takes time, and trying to rush the process often leads to burnout and an abandonment of promising practices. Include time for learning, adjusting, and celebrating small wins along the way.

STEP 4: Implement systematically.

Focus on what you can control directly in your classroom and immediate work area. Support colleagues who want to try new approaches by sharing resources, co-teaching lessons, or listening when they need to process challenging situations.

Advocate for consistent approaches by pointing out specific examples of what's working and what's creating confusion for students. *Offer solutions, not just problems.*

If you're in a leadership position, work to align practices gradually. If not, model trauma-responsive approaches and let the results speak for themselves.

Start with high-impact, low-effort changes that demonstrate quick wins, such as adjusting how you respond to one specific behavior, changing your morning greeting routine, or modifying how you handle transitions. These visible successes generate credibility for larger systemic changes later.

STEP 5: Create consistent practices across all settings and build lasting change.

Work within your sphere of influence to create consistency. If you're a classroom teacher, focus on your grade-level team. If you're a specialist, work to align with classroom practices. If you're an administrator, coordinate building-wide approaches. Document what's working through before-and-after observations, student feedback, or caregiver comments. Share these success stories to increase support for continued implementation. Plan for sustainability by training multiple people to use your successful strategies, and connect with community resources and professional networks to stay current with best practices.

Remember: This process typically takes two to three years to see significant school-wide change. Focus on progress, not perfection.

OVERCOMING PUSHBACK

When you begin advocating for school-wide trauma-responsive practices, you'll encounter predictable concerns from colleagues, administrators, and community members who are more comfortable with existing approaches. Here's how to address the most common forms of resistance while staying committed to creating healing environments for all students.

We don't have time for another initiative. Frame trauma-responsive practices as a way to make existing work more effective. Show colleagues how these approaches can reduce the time they currently spend on behavior management, parent conferences about disciplinary issues, and classroom disruptions. Teachers can spot a time-wasting initiative from three hallways away. We've developed supernatural powers for detecting anything that adds to our already impossible to-do lists. Share specific examples of how trauma-responsive strategies have made teaching more manageable and effective for you and others.

Trauma-responsive teaching is the latest fad that will be replaced next year. Acknowledge that education does tend to cycle through trends, but explain that trauma-responsive practices are grounded in decades of neuroscience research about how children learn and develop. Point out that these approaches align with timeless educational values like building relationships, understanding individual needs, and creating safe learning environments.

Some of these kids need firm boundaries and consequences. Yes, all students need clear expectations and consistent responses, and trauma-responsive practices provide both structure and support. Help colleagues understand that being trauma-responsive doesn't mean being permissive; it means responding to behavior in ways that teach rather than punish while maintaining high expectations for all students.

Parents expect us to be strict and hold kids accountable. Most parents want their children to be successful, feel safe, and develop positive relationships with adults. Share examples of how trauma-responsive approaches have led to improved behavior, better academic outcomes, and stronger school-home partnerships. When parents see that these practices help their children thrive, they become advocates for this method.

Administration won't support this because it's too expensive. Many trauma-responsive practices require minimal financial investment because they're about changing approaches rather than purchasing programs. Start with cost-neutral strategies like policy revisions, staff collaboration, and modified procedures. Document the positive outcomes to gather support for any financial investments that might be helpful later.

It's not fair for us to treat some kids differently from others. Help people understand the difference between equal treatment and equitable treatment. Explain that fairness means giving each student what they need to be successful, not giving everyone identical responses. Use analogies like providing wheelchairs for students who have difficulty walking on their own or allowing extra time for students with learning differences.

THE HACK IN ACTION

Liberty Oaks Elementary School had struggled for years with high suspension rates, teacher turnover, and low academic achievement. The building served a diverse community where nearly 80 percent of students qualified for free or reduced lunch, and many families faced housing instability, deployment cycles, and other stressors that impacted their children's ability to focus on learning.

PreK teacher Mrs. Lilly had been implementing trauma-responsive practices in her classroom for two years, with remarkable results. Her students showed significant growth, behavioral incidents decreased dramatically, and families regularly commented on the positive changes they saw at home. But Mrs. Lilly was exhausted from constantly advocating for her students after they left her classroom and encountered inconsistent responses throughout the school.

The turning point came during a particularly challenging week when two of Mrs. Lilly's students were suspended for behaviors that occurred outside of her classroom—one incident happened during PE class, and the other occurred in the cafeteria during lunch. These were behaviors she recognized as trauma responses, but they were handled punitively by staff who hadn't learned these approaches.

Instead of accepting the status quo, Mrs. Lilly approached her principal with a proposal. She offered to share what she'd learned about trauma-responsive teaching with interested colleagues and requested permission to form a voluntary study group.

Principal Harjo was initially skeptical but agreed to let Mrs. Lilly try. The first meeting attracted only three other teachers, but Mrs. Lilly came prepared with specific examples of how trauma-responsive strategies had helped actual students they all knew. She shared stories of improved behavior, increased engagement, and stronger family relationships that resulted from understanding rather than punishing trauma responses.

Word spread gradually as these four teachers began collaborating regularly and sharing strategies. The school counselor asked to join the group, followed by two paraprofessionals who worked with many of the same students. Within six months, the study group had grown to include twelve staff members representing every grade level and several support positions.

The group's influence extended beyond their monthly meetings. Teachers began informally consulting each other about challenging situations, and they shared resources and advocated collectively for students who needed additional support. They started using a common language about trauma responses and consistent approaches to behavior support.

Principal Harjo noticed the changes before he fully understood what was causing them. Office referrals from participating teachers decreased significantly, while parent feedback about those classrooms became increasingly positive. When he asked Mrs. Lilly to explain what was happening, she invited him to attend one of their collaborative meetings.

That invitation transformed the initiative from a grassroots teacher effort into a school-wide priority. Principal Harjo became convinced that trauma-responsive practices weren't just effective— they were essential for serving the student population. He began providing release time for teachers to observe each other's classrooms, brought in expert training for the entire staff, and worked with the team to revise school policies that inadvertently retraumatized vulnerable students.

The changes weren't immediate or dramatic, but they were sustained and meaningful. Over two years, Liberty Oaks Elementary saw a 70 percent reduction in out-of-school suspensions, a significant decrease in teacher turnover, and steady improvements in academic achievement across all grade levels. Also, the school developed a reputation in the community as a place where all children could feel safe, supported, and successful.

Mrs. Lilly's classroom success had become the catalyst for a comprehensive school transformation, but the lasting change happened because trauma-responsive practices became embedded in the culture and operations of the entire building. Teachers supported each other, administrators aligned policies with values, and families felt genuinely welcomed and valued.

At Roosevelt High School, the transformation looked different but followed similar principles. English teacher Mr. Johnson had been struggling with what seemed like increasingly disrespectful and disengaged students in his ninth-grade classes. Traditional classroom management strategies weren't working, and he was seriously considering leaving teaching altogether.

Everything changed when Mr. Johnson attended a summer institute on trauma-responsive education. He returned to school that fall with a new understanding of how adverse childhood experiences affect adolescent behavior and learning. He began recognizing that what he'd interpreted as defiance was often dys-regulation, and what looked like laziness might be students feeling overwhelmed or struggling with executive function challenges.

He started small by changing his responses to student behavior and incorporating more choice and flexibility into his class-room procedures. The results were encouraging enough that he began sharing his experiences with colleagues in his professional learning community.

Biology teacher Ms. Higa was initially skeptical but became interested when Mr. Johnson described specific strategies that had helped students she also taught. Drama teacher Mr. Nakamura joined their conversations after seeing improvements in the behavior and engagement of the students they shared.

The three teachers began meeting regularly to share resources, problem-solve challenges, and support each other's implementa-tion of trauma-responsive practices. With administrative support, they were occasionally able to team-teach when floaters covered their classes, allowing them to observe different approaches and provide mutual feedback.

Their collaboration caught the attention of their department heads, who asked them to present their strategies to the broader faculty. The presentation generated enough interest that the school administration provided funding for comprehensive trauma-responsive training for all staff.

The school-wide implementation at Roosevelt High took three years and faced significant resistance from some veteran teachers who believed that trauma-responsive approaches would lower academic standards. However, evidence of improved grades, decreased disciplinary incidents, and higher graduation rates among at-risk students gradually won over the skeptics.

By the fourth year, Roosevelt High had become a model for trauma-responsive secondary education in the district. The transformation happened because one teacher's success led to the formation of collaborative teams, which, in turn, influenced school policies and created sustainable systems change.

Creating trauma-responsive schools requires moving beyond individual classroom efforts toward comprehensive, collaborative approaches that transform entire educational communities. While dedicated teachers can create healing spaces within their classrooms, lasting change for vulnerable students requires consistency, support, and alignment across all school settings.

The most effective transformations begin with small groups of committed educators who are willing to share their experiences, learn from each other, and advocate collectively for policy changes that support children affected by trauma. These collaborative teams become the foundation for broader professional development, systemic policy revision, and cultural shifts that benefit all students.

School-wide trauma-responsive implementation is about creating environments where trauma-responsive approaches become the natural way of doing business because they make sense, they work, and they're supported at every level of the organization.

The investment required—in time, training, and sometimes resources—pays dividends for students who have experienced trauma and for the entire school community. When adults understand behavior as communication, respond to needs rather than symptoms, and work together to support students' success, everyone benefits.

All students, and especially those who have been in the foster care system and others with complex trauma histories, deserve schools where every adult understands their needs and responds with competence and compassion. They deserve an educational environment where all children can develop resilience, form positive relationships, and achieve their potential.

We can't continue to expect isolated teachers to carry the full weight of supporting students exposed to trauma while navigating systems that inadvertently punish and retraumatize the children who need safety the most. The village that raises our most vulnerable children must include every adult who touches their lives during the school day.

The time for half-measures and individual heroics has passed. Our students deserve comprehensive, collaborative approaches that transform schools into communities of care where every child can heal, learn, and thrive.

REFLECTION
QUESTIONS

1. **Who are your potential allies in creating trauma-responsive practices at your school?** Think beyond obvious candidates to include support staff, specialists, and administrators who might be interested in this work.

2. **What school policies or procedures might inadvertently retraumatize vulnerable students?** Consider discipline policies, grading practices, homework expectations, and family engagement requirements.

3. **How could you share your trauma-responsive successes in ways that inspire rather than intimidate colleagues?** Focus on specific strategies and student outcomes rather than theoretical concepts.

4. **What would whole-school trauma-responsive implementation look like in your context?** Consider your student population, staff culture, administrative support, and community characteristics.

CONCLUSION

EMBRACE YOUR NEW ROLE AS A TRAUMA-RESPONSIVE EDUCATOR

Transform Education
One Classroom at a Time

*Education is not preparation for
life; education is life itself.*
— JOHN DEWEY, EDUCATOR AND PHILOSOPHER

SIX MONTHS FROM now, you might find yourself in a moment that takes your breath away. Maybe it will be watching a student who used to shut down completely raise her hand for the first time. Perhaps it will be seeing a child who once lived in constant survival mode peacefully reading in your classroom's cozy corner. It could be receiving a note from a parent, thanking you for seeing their child's strengths when everyone else focused on deficits.

These moments don't happen by accident. They happen because you chose to see behavior as communication. Because you decided that relationships come before rigor. Because you created spaces where every child can feel safe, valued, and capable of growth.

The Ripple Effects of Trauma-Responsive Teaching

When you implement these ten Hacks, you're moving beyond changing individual classroom practices and participating in a fundamental shift in how education approaches human development. The student who learns to self-regulate in your classroom carries those skills into every future relationship. The child who discovers his strengths in your room develops a sense of identity that sustains him through life's challenges. The family that feels truly welcomed by your empathetic approach begins to see school as a partner rather than a place of judgment.

But the ripples extend even further. Your colleagues notice the calm energy in your classroom and start asking questions. School leaders see reduced discipline referrals and improved engagement. Other educators begin experimenting with trauma-responsive approaches. What started as your individual commitment to seeing students differently becomes a movement that transforms entire school cultures.

Consider Ms. Lau, a second-grade teacher who began this journey by simply removing her behavior chart. Within weeks, she noticed students taking more risks in their learning, conflicts resolving more quickly, and parents expressing gratitude for positive communication. By the end of the year, three other teachers had made similar changes. The next year, the entire grade level adopted trauma-responsive practices. Today, Ms. Lau's school is known district-wide for its healing-centered approach to education.

These Practices Benefit All Students

One of the most powerful aspects of trauma-responsive teaching is that you don't need to know which students have experienced trauma to implement these approaches effectively. The strategies in this book aren't special accommodations for "broken" children—they're evidence-based practices that help *every* brain learn more effectively.

When you create predictable, calming environments, every student benefits from reduced anxiety. When you offer choices and build on strengths, all learners become more engaged and motivated. When you prioritize relationships and co-regulation, every child develops stronger social-emotional skills. The student who seems to have it all together may be carrying invisible stress that your trauma-responsive practices help address. The child who appears confident may be masking deep insecurity that your strengths-based approach begins to heal.

This universal applicability means you can implement these Hacks without singling out particular students or requiring extensive trauma histories. You're simply creating the conditions where all brains can thrive, all bodies can feel safe, and all hearts can remain open to learning.

Start Where You Are and Build Momentum

You don't need to overhaul your entire teaching practice overnight. The beauty of these ten Hacks lies in their accessibility. Each one offers immediate actions you can take tomorrow alongside long-term visions for transformation.

Maybe you start by changing your physical environment, swapping harsh fluorescent lights for soft lamps and creating a calming corner where students can regulate. Perhaps you begin with mindset shifts, consciously reframing one challenging behavior each day as communication. You might focus on relationships first, implementing daily connection rituals that help you truly know your students as whole people.

Trust yourself to know what feels most urgent in your current context. If you're overwhelmed by behavioral challenges, Hack 1's approach to seeing behavior as communication might be your starting point. If you're working with students who have internalized deficit messages, Hack 2's strengths-based focus could be transformative. If your school culture feels punitive, beginning with Hack 3's dismantling of public shaming systems might create the biggest impact.

The key is to maintain consistency rather than perfection. Small, sustained changes create more lasting transformation than dramatic overhauls that prove impossible to maintain. Give yourself permission to grow slowly, make mistakes, and celebrate progress.

This work is as much about your healing and growth as it is about serving students. As you practice co-regulation, you develop your emotional intelligence. As you design predictable environments, you create the stability you need as an educator. As you focus on strengths, you begin to see your assets more clearly.

Sustain Your Commitment

Trauma-responsive teaching requires emotional and mental resources that traditional approaches don't demand. You'll need strategies for sustaining this work without burning out. Include consistent self-care practices that help you regulate your nervous system. Seek out colleagues who share your commitment to healing-centered education. Advocate for systemic changes that support trauma-responsive practices at the administrative level.

You can't heal trauma that isn't yours to heal, but you can create conditions where healing becomes possible. You're not responsible for fixing every student's challenges, but you are responsible for ensuring that your classroom becomes a place where growth and recovery can occur.

Your Ongoing Learning Journey

This book represents the beginning of your trauma-responsive journey. Continue deepening your understanding through ongoing professional development, research, and reflection. Consider these resources for continued growth:

- **Books:** Explore works by Dr. Bruce Perry, Dr. Lori Desautels, Dr. Barbara Sorrels, Dr. Dan Siegel, and Kristin Souers for a deeper understanding of trauma and brain science.

- **Training:** Seek trauma-informed care certification through organizations like the National Child Traumatic Stress Network.

- **Communities:** Join professional learning networks focused on trauma-responsive education.

- **Reflection:** Maintain a teaching journal where you document successes, challenges, and insights from implementing these practices.

The Invitation Forward

Your students are waiting for you—not a perfect version of you, but the you who's willing to see them fully, respond to them thoughtfully, and believe in their inherent worth and capabilities. They need educators who understand that behavior is communication, that every child carries both struggles and strengths, and that healing happens in relationship.

You already have everything you need to begin:

- Your willingness to question traditional approaches and imagine a better way.

- Your commitment to seeing each student as a whole person deserving of dignity and respect.

- Your belief that education can be a force for healing.

The work won't always be easy. There will be days when nothing seems to work, when you question whether these approaches are making a difference, or when the weight of students' pain feels overwhelming. In those moments, remember that transformation rarely happens in straight lines. Every small act of compassion, every moment of genuine connection, every time you choose understanding over punishment, you are planting seeds that may not bloom until long after students leave your classroom.

But they *will* bloom. The students who learned to trust adults in your room will form healthier relationships throughout their lives. The children who discovered their strengths in your classroom will draw on that knowledge during future challenges. The family that felt welcomed in your space will approach their next educational experience with greater hope and engagement.

This scenario is the ripple effect of trauma-responsive teaching. It is how individual educators create system-wide change. It is how we transform education from a place where some children survive to a space where all children thrive.

Your journey as a trauma-responsive educator starts now. Take one step, then another. Trust the process. Celebrate the small victories. And remember—you're not just teaching subjects or managing behaviors. You're participating in the sacred work of helping human beings discover their capacity for resilience, growth, and connection.

The children who need you the most are waiting. They're ready for you to see their behavior as communication, to build on their strengths, and to create safety and predictability in their learning environment. They're ready for an adult who believes in their ability to heal and grow.

Are you ready to be that adult for them?

Every child who enters your classroom brings a story. Some stories include trauma, loss, and pain. But every story also includes strength, resilience, and hope. Your job isn't to rewrite their stories; it's to create conditions where they can author their next chapters with confidence, dignity, and joy.

That's the promise and possibility of trauma-responsive education.

Let's continue.

ABOUT THE AUTHORS

DR. KATIE FIELDS is a visiting assistant professor of education at the University of Central Oklahoma, where she teaches undergraduate and graduate teacher preparation courses. She holds a doctorate in Instructional Leadership and Academic Curriculum with an emphasis in Early Childhood Education from the University of Oklahoma, a master's degree in Early Childhood Education from Northeastern State University, and a bachelor's degree in Early Childhood Education from the University of Oklahoma.

With nine years of classroom teaching experience spanning age three through fourth grade, and three years as a professor, Katie brings both practical and theoretical expertise to her work. She previously served as director of the Child Development Center at the University of Science and Arts of Oklahoma, where she gained valuable experience in early childhood program leadership.

Katie's research focuses on trauma-responsive practices and teachers as advocates, with a particular emphasis on her groundbreaking trauma-*plus* framework for understanding the unique educational needs of children who have been in the foster care system.

She has presented her work at numerous local, state, and national conferences on topics including teacher advocacy, trauma-responsive practices, working with foster children, and multiage classrooms. Her research has been published in national journals, including *Action in Teacher Education* and *Teaching and Teacher Education*.

An active member of NAEYC, NAECTE, OkAEYC, and OAECTE (where she serves as secretary/treasurer), Katie is committed to advancing the early childhood education profession through advocacy and research. What drives her work is simple: wanting to do better and be better for her students so they can be better for their students, ultimately improving education and transforming lives.

Katie and her husband, Ben, have been foster parents for over two years, an experience that has deepened her commitment to trauma-responsive education. They have two adult children, Angel and Joey. When she's not teaching, researching, or advocating, Katie enjoys reading and playing video games, often with her pittie princess Noelle by her side. Connect with her at www.drkatiefields.com and on Facebook and LinkedIn under Dr. Katie Fields.

DR. JILL M. DAVIS is a professor of education at the University of Central Oklahoma, where she teaches undergraduate and graduate teacher preparation courses. She holds a doctorate in Instructional Leadership and Academic Curriculum from the University of Oklahoma–Tulsa, and a master's degree and bachelor's degree in Early Childhood Education from Northeastern State University.

With thirteen years of experience as a public school early childhood teacher, Jill brings a trauma-responsive, constructivist lens to her work. She is dedicated to preparing both pre-service and practicing educators to support children's social-emotional development in an increasingly academic-focused landscape.

Jill's research and writing focus on advocacy as a pathway to equity, whether through trauma-responsive practices, developmentally appropriate instruction, or student-centered early childhood mathematics. Her work centers on empowering educators as catalysts for change, equipping them to lead with confidence, influence policy, and challenge systemic barriers that impact children, families, and the profession.

A frequent presenter at national, state, and local conferences, Jill bridges research and practice to inspire meaningful action.

Her mission is to help educators find their voices as advocates and create learning environments where both teachers and children can thrive.

When she is not teaching, writing, or advocating, Jill enjoys crafting, crossword puzzles, and game nights with her husband and two children. Connect with her at www.drjilldavis.net and on Facebook and LinkedIn under the username Dr. Jill Davis.

ACKNOWLEDGMENTS

Katie:

We stand on the shoulders of giants in trauma-responsive education, and I want to acknowledge the pioneering researchers whose foundational work made this book possible. Dr. Bruce Perry's groundbreaking research on trauma and brain development, Dr. Karyn Purvis's Trust-Based Relational Intervention work, and Dr. Barbara Sorrels's practical applications of trauma-responsive practices in educational settings have shaped our understanding and informed our approach throughout this work. Their dedication to understanding and supporting children affected by trauma has paved the way for all of us working in this field.

Thank you to the team at Times 10 Publications for believing in this project and supporting us throughout the writing process.

To my co-author, colleague, and friend, Dr. Jill Davis. Your wisdom, humor, and unwavering commitment to this work made every aspect of this collaboration a joy. Thank you for pushing us both to think deeper, for bringing clarity to complex ideas, and for making this book stronger through our partnership. Working with you has been one of the greatest privileges of my professional life.

To the foster children who have shared their lives with our family. You have been my greatest teachers, showing me resilience I never knew was possible and inspiring me to become not just a better educator, but a better human being. Your courage, strength, and capacity for healing in the face of unimaginable challenges continue to motivate everything I do. This work exists because of you and for you.

To the educators who have trusted me with their questions, challenges, and successes. Thank you for your willingness to grow, change, and put children's needs first, even when it's difficult. Your dedication to trauma-responsive practices gives me hope for every child who walks into a classroom.

To my children, Angel and Joey. You have watched me pursue this passion for years, cheering me on through graduate school, research projects, and now this book. Thank you for your patience with my endless foster care advocacy, your understanding when work consumed too many evenings (and let's be honest, too many dinner conversations), and your unwavering belief that this work matters. I am so proud of the compassionate adults you have become.

And finally, to my husband, Ben. For twenty-six years, you have been my anchor, my cheerleader, and my voice of reason. You've supported every wild idea, every late-night writing session, and every child in the foster care system who has needed our home. Your steady love and unshakable faith in me made this book (and everything else) possible. Thank you for walking this journey beside me with such strength and love.

Jill:

Thank you to the team at Times 10 Publications for your encouragement and support throughout this process.

To my co-author and long-time friend, Dr. Katie Fields. Your energy, persistence, and partnership turned this book from an idea into reality. From student to colleague, it has been an honor to grow and create with you. We made the Dream Team come to life.

To all my students, from pre-kindergarten to graduate school. You've challenged me, inspired me, and taught me more than you'll ever know. Thank you for letting me learn alongside you and reminding me why this work matters.

To the teachers who helped me discover my calling: Mrs. Judy

Bliss, Professor Jack Gleason, Dr. Libby Ethridge, Dr. Vickie Lake, and so many others. Your belief in me made all the difference.

To the educators I have worked with over the years, from the Kendall-Whittier crew to the C&I team. Thank you for your wisdom and collaboration. Special thanks to Dr. Darlinda Cassel for your thoughtful conversations and steady encouragement, Dr. Keith Higa for a decade of well-timed humor and perfectly placed sarcasm that helped me keep things in perspective, and Dr. Dan Vincent for being the best department chair ever. Your mentorship, empathy, podcast-worthy wisdom, and unwavering support have inspired me to grow every day.

To my sister, Melena, my first teacher. You taught me to read, setting me on the path to becoming a lifelong learner. I wouldn't be where I am today without you and your collection of Little Golden Books.

To my children, Alden and Sylvia. One of you is off unlocking new levels, the other is still humming through the overture. You've shown me that the best adventures include both power-ups and power ballads. Thank you for reminding me that whether we're navigating boss fights or belting out big finales, the real magic is in the journey we share.

And, finally, to my husband, Joe. For thirty-two years, you have been my steady companion through every step of this odyssey, including the tight spots and muddy detours. You have stood beside me at every crossroad with love, humor, patience, and support. You are the real treasure and always have been bona fide.

SNEAK PEEK

HACK 6

Assess the Situation Before Jumping In

Determine Why Students Are Academically Struggling

It is a capital mistake to theorize before one has data.

— SIR ARTHUR CONAN DOYLE,
AUTHOR, VIA SHERLOCK HOLMES

THE PROBLEM
THE SAME STUDENTS ALWAYS NEED RESCUE SUPPORT

When the same students need rescue support, everyone is impacted. Just as turbulent waves affect beachgoers and lifeguards, academic difficulties create riptides that threaten to drown some students and those around them.

The first person affected is the student. Their academic challenges not only impact their performance during school but also outside of it. Students who underperform find it difficult to understand new content, complete assignments, and do well on assessments, leading to negative self-perceptions. As a result, they may become disengaged in class discussions and reluctant to participate in group activities, fearing they might not appear as smart as their classmates. Persistent struggles also take a toll on their emotions, contributing to increased stress, anxiety, and frustration both in and out of school. Additionally, many must spend extra time studying for tests and completing their assignments at home, leaving less time for school activities and socializing with their friends.

Parents and guardians of such students also experience emotional challenges. They worry about their child's academic performance, increasing their own stress and anxiety levels. Consistent academic struggles can also impact family dynamics, leading to tension and conflicts between parents and their children. Some parents may even question their parenting abilities. To overcome feelings of guilt, parents might feel obligated to seek additional support outside of school, such as hiring tutors or purchasing online educational programs. These extra expenses can put a financial strain on families with limited resources.

When the same students repeatedly face academic challenges, the impact extends to the entire class, as teachers must adjust their instructional pace, resulting in superficial coverage or teaching less content. Other students' engagement might suffer due to interruptions caused by giving extra attention to students who need it. Balancing individualized support and whole-class instruction can be challenging for teachers, and it leads to an increased workload and potential burnout.

School and district leaders are also affected in several ways by students who consistently struggle. When students struggle in the classroom, they often become disruptive or disengaged, which can increase office referrals and add to the workload for principals. Repeated office referrals can strain relationships and create feelings of discouragement for both administrators and students. Moreover, these students' academic performance affects overall achievement levels, leading to lower scores on state assessments and potentially affecting the reputation of the school and district.

THE HACK
ASSESS THE SITUATION BEFORE JUMPING IN

We've all done it. When a tooth hurts, we take a pain reliever and hope the pain goes away. In most cases, the medication only masks the problem, and when the pain continues, we eventually make an appointment with our dentist to determine the root cause of the problem.

Determine why the same students often struggle and work to prevent future academic emergencies from occurring.

It can be tempting to address problems by putting an intervention in place before the causes are known, but as we know, that doesn't usually fix the problem. When the same students need rescue support, the answer isn't to simply add more lifeguards. We risk overloading our learning lifeguarding system if we don't investigate the causes to determine why the same students are consistently struggling. Delving deeper into instructional and assessment practices to identify root causes can help educators select and implement solutions that produce better results.

WHAT YOU CAN DO TOMORROW

While lifeguards near swimming areas are trained in a variety of rescue techniques to assist swimmers in difficult situations, their goal is to prevent incidents from occurring in the first place. They are taught to effectively scan a body of water and its surrounding area to prevent and respond to emergencies. The ideas described in this section are primarily designed to help teachers quickly determine why the same students often struggle and work to prevent future academic emergencies from occurring.

⟡ Use pre-assessments to detect rough waters.

Administering low-stakes diagnostic assessments before teaching each unit can help teachers determine the knowledge and skills that students bring into the classroom and detect potential trouble spots.

- When introducing pre-assessments, help students understand that the information collected won't affect their course grades. Instead, convey that the assessments are a great way for students to find out what they will be learning and to understand that if they put forth their best effort, the assessments will help them recognize their strengths and alert them to challenging content so they can ask for help when the time comes.
- Unit pre-assessments should target crucial prerequisite understandings, knowledge, and skills, and they should align with the unit's priority standards.
- Assessments must be brief (just a few questions) so the data can be quickly gathered and analyzed.
- Pre-assessment data is most useful when the assessments are administered a week or two before introducing each unit, allowing teachers time to pinpoint misconceptions and assess missing prerequisite knowledge and skills.

✛ Employ active participation strategies.

Create a classroom culture where participation is expected. Assessment expert Dylan Wiliam, in his book *Embedded Formative Assessment*, argues that when teachers exclusively call on students who raise their hands, they actually widen the achievement gap. Participating students get smarter, and learners who refrain from interacting miss out on their chance to improve their abilities.

Requiring students to frequently respond to instruction through oral, written, and action responses will keep them engaged in the learning process, reduce behavioral challenges, and help identify students who may need additional support. Cold calling, a response strategy explained by Doug Lemov in *Teach Like a Champion*, has proven especially effective.

- The key to cold calling is to establish the routine and build support so all students feel comfortable participating. This can be done by informing students that you will be cold calling before lecturing, reading a passage, or watching a video.
- You can also provide extra prep time by letting specific students know in advance that you will be calling on them.
- Providing opportunities for students to check their answers through turn and talks or think-write-pair-share activities can boost the confidence of shy or reluctant students.
- When requiring frequent responses, give students adequate thinking time so they don't feel rushed. Processing the answer in your own head when students are formulating their answers and having students write their answers on paper or individual whiteboards are a couple of strategies teachers can use to reduce guessing and give students more time to formulate their answers.

Early detection of misconceptions and errors can prevent or reduce academic tragedies. To fully reap the benefits of active participation strategies, teachers can engage with the answers they receive by asking additional probing questions and following up with students whose errors or misconceptions indicate that reteaching may be necessary.

Deepen engagement through quizzing.

When students view assessment as a learning opportunity, it provides even greater benefits. The routine use of low-stakes quizzes can guide whole-class instruction and help teachers quickly gauge which students may be confused or struggling to apply the content and concepts.

Our brains are constantly recording information temporarily. When the content doesn't appear again, it is often forgotten. Without refreshers, newly learned information fades away within days. Routine quizzing provides ongoing opportunities for retrieval practice, and studies have shown this assessment practice can promote student learning and engagement.

When designing quizzes, select a format that is short and informative. Multiple-choice questions are easy to grade but also encourage guessing. Consider alternatives that provide deeper insights into what students are thinking. Short-answer questions or quick-writes encourage students to move beyond merely recalling facts.

The routine use of quizzes that incorporate various design features and methods can promote deeper engagement with the content. They also provide teachers and students with feedback that proactively promotes learning as opposed to taking reactionary measures when students become disengaged or fail. The following are a few options for presenting quizzes.

- *Quizzing before class:* Quizzing students at the start of class can be a great way to quickly identify the concepts from the previous day's lesson that are giving students the most trouble. Depending on the assessment results, teachers can either address misconceptions immediately with the entire class or note which students would benefit from timely reteaching in a small group or one-on-one instructional setting.

- *Quizzing with partners:* Collaborative quizzing can promote an interactive and engaging learning environment, generate enthusiastic discussions, and include real-life simulations of how successful individuals often draw on the expertise of others to complete tasks or solve problems. With this strategy, students take a short quiz, turn over their papers, and discuss the quiz content with a partner (or small group). Then, they return to their quiz and may change their answers, if desired, before submitting it.

- *Quizzing with resources:* Daily open-note quizzes can help students solidify key concepts and promote effective note-taking and organizational skills. When students locate the answer in their notes—they actually read their notes!

- *Quizzing with technology:* With this strategy, students complete an online quiz using Google Forms, a learning management system, or individual response devices such as clickers. In both examples, teachers can quickly identify areas of misunderstanding and address the concepts that are giving students the most trouble.

- *Quizzing after questioning:* Before administering a quiz, students ask clarifying questions about the most recently taught material. Then, the students and the teacher work together to discuss and find answers to these questions. If many good questions are asked, discussed, and answered by various students, the teacher may choose to skip the quiz. This approach pushes students to engage with the content on a deeper level and teaches them how to ask insightful questions.

- *Quizzing after class:* Quizzing students at the end of class provides teachers with immediate feedback on the effectiveness of their instruction and identifies which students may benefit from additional instruction and practice before the next day's lesson.

Actively monitor all learners.

By closely observing their students' behaviors and interactions in class, teachers can gain valuable insight into who may be falling behind in their learning. If students appear restless, agitated, uncertain, or distracted, they may find it difficult to comprehend the material. Additionally, limited participation in class discussions or group work may indicate they have lost confidence in themselves as learners. Scheduling one-on-one conversations to learn more about their underlying issues will build rapport with students and improve their chances of academic success.

MORE FROM TIMES 10 PUBLICATIONS

Hacking School Discipline TOGETHER
10 Ways to Create a Culture of Empathy and Responsibility Using Schoolwide Restorative Justice

By Jeffrey Benson

This sequel to *Hacking School Discipline* is for teachers, administrators, and staff who long to create a school that fosters responsibility, forgiveness, and accountability so students can learn from their impulsive decisions. We can change the status quo and create a school where administrators and staff trust each other, and students benefit from what we do best: educate.

The Lifeguard

Building Relationships & Supporting Students: An Illustrated Story

By Sherri Nelson

The Lifeguard is a powerful, true-to-life story about Maya, a student battling trauma, poverty, and academic failure. Witness what it means to be a learning lifeguard and see how a team of committed educators comes together to throw lifelines, build trust, and help Maya believe in her future. *Wall Street Journal* bestselling author Damon West calls it "your invitation to dive in," reminding us that ordinary people can make an extraordinary impact.

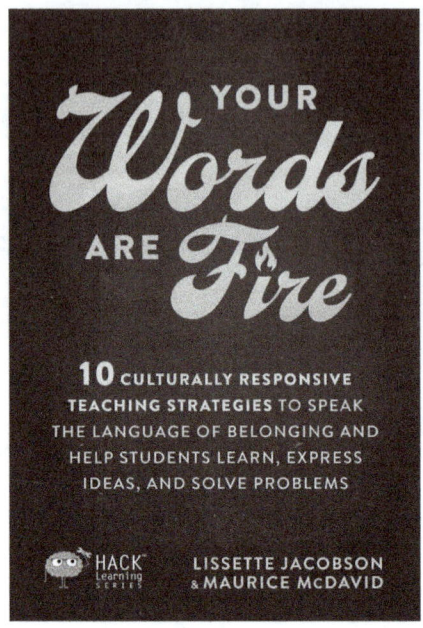

Your Words Are Fire

10 Culturally Responsive Teaching Strategies to Speak the
Language of Belonging and Help Students Learn, Express Ideas,
and Solve Problems

By Lissette Jacobson and Maurice McDavid

Language—how we use it and what we think about it—can help or
hinder our students' high-level learning, especially kids from culturally and linguistically diverse backgrounds. These ten teaching strategies can build a bridge between the languages your students are using
and the languages they need for academic success, while supporting
their cultural and linguistic identities.

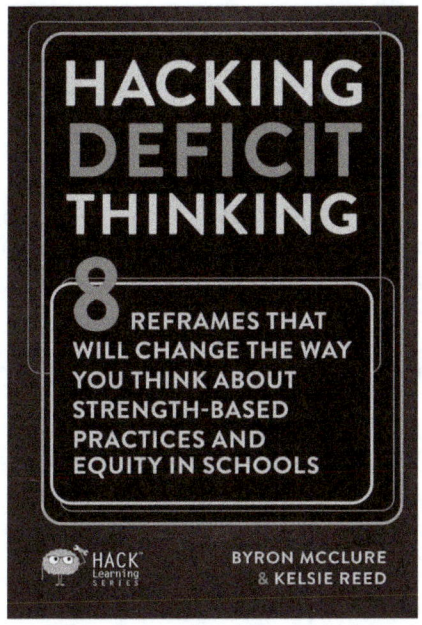

Hacking Deficit Thinking

8 Reframes That Will Change the Way You Think about Strength-Based Practices and Equity in Schools

By Byron McClure and Kelsie Reed

Too many teachers focus on what's wrong with their students instead of what's strong. A focus on weakness is a pervasive, powerful judgment that harms students long after they leave school. It's time for educators to reframe teaching and learning. McClure and Reed show how to unlearn student blame and reframe thinking to focus on students' strengths, benefiting them for life.

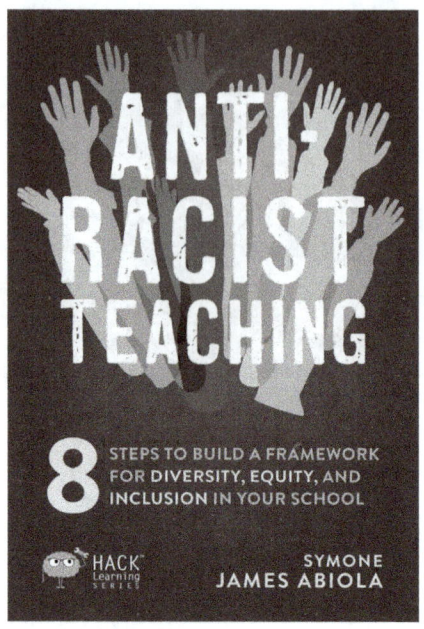

Anti-Racist Teaching

8 Steps to Build a Framework for Diversity, Equity, and Inclusion in Your School

By Symone James Abiola

Believing that racism is wrong is not enough; we must take action to address racial inequities within schools. As educators, engaging in the foundational work of addressing racial inequity and uplifting all students is our highest responsibility to the students and families we serve. Use this guide to address the impact of racism and bias in your school and provide an empowering experience for all students.

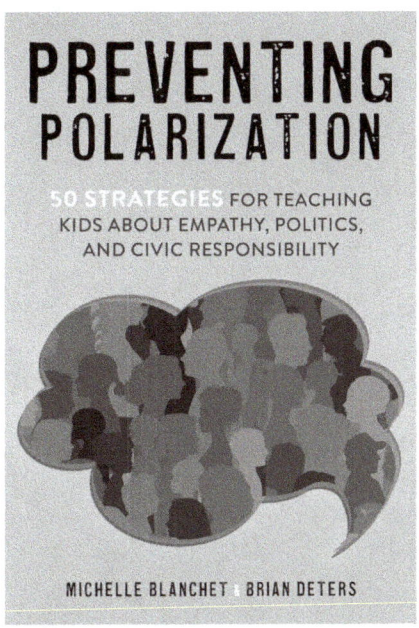

Preventing Polarization

50 Strategies for Teaching Kids about Empathy, Politics, and Civic Responsibility

By Michelle Blanchet and Brian Deters

In an era that has become incredibly polarized politically and socially, we can help our students come together despite differences and become active and engaged citizens. A one-off civics course is not enough. Learn essential strategies to create experiences that help students break down barriers through activities and role-playing. Let's show our students how to make a difference, minimize conflict, and build accord.

www.ingramcontent.com/pod-product-compliance
Lightning Source LLC
Chambersburg PA
CBHW061607120626
46550CB00004B/1638

TIMES 10 PUBLICATIONS provides practical solutions that busy people can read today and use tomorrow. We bring you content from experienced researchers and practitioners, and we share it through books, podcasts, webinars, articles, events, and ongoing conversations on social media. Our books and materials help turn practice into action.

Stay in touch with us at HackLearningLife.com and 10Publications.com and follow our updates @10Publications.